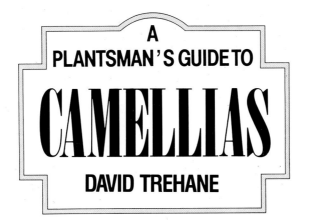

A
PLANTSMAN'S GUIDE TO
CAMELLIAS

DAVID TREHANE

A
PLANTSMAN'S GUIDE TO
CAMELLIAS

DAVID TREHANE

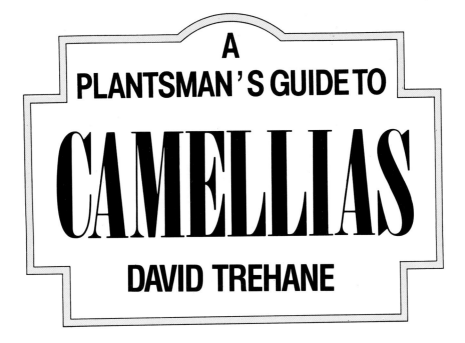

SERIES EDITOR
ALAN TOOGOOD

WARD LOCK

Text © Ward Lock Ltd 1990
Line drawings © Ward Lock Ltd 1990

First published in Great Britain in 1990
by Ward Lock Limited, Artillery House,
Artillery Row, London SW1P 1RT, a Cassell
Company

House editor Denis Ingram

Text filmset in Times
by Dorchester Typesetting
Printed and bound in Portugal
by Resopal

British Library Cataloguing in Publication Data
Trehane, David
    A plantsman's guide to Camellias.
    1. Gardens. Camellias
    I. Title
    635.9'33166

ISBN 0 7063 6835 5

CONTENTS

Editor's Foreword □ 11

PUBLISHER'S NOTE

Readers are requested to note that in order to make the text intelligible in both hemispheres, plant flowering times, etc. are described in terms of seasons, not months. The following table provides an approximate 'translation' of seasons into months for the two hemispheres.

Northern Hemisphere		Southern Hemisphere
Mid-winter	= January	= Mid-summer
Late winter	= February	= Late summer
Early spring	= March	= Early autumn
Mid-spring	= April	= Mid-autumn
Late spring	= May	= Late autumn
Early summer	= June	= Early winter
Mid-summer	= July	= Mid-winter
Late summer	= August	= Late winter
Early autumn	= September	= Early spring
Mid-autumn	= October	= Mid-spring
Late autumn	= November	= Late spring
Early winter	= December	= Early summer

Captions for colour photographs on chapter opening pages:

Pp. 12–13 A typical Cornish planting of mixed camellias in the renowned garden of Trengwainton, Penzance.

Pp. 20–21 The full peony × *williamsii* 'Debbie' in association with *Rhododendron* 'Blue Diamond'.

Pp. 42–43 A homely scene for any garden on acid soil: camellias in a sheltered corner.

Pp. 92–93 'Donation', the unfailing archetype of the hardy × *williamsii* camellias.

Pp. 110–111 In Britain the strong-growing 'Adolphe Audusson' is the most freely planted red *japonica* camellia.

EDITOR'S FOREWORD

This unique series takes a completely fresh look at the most popular garden and greenhouse plants.

Written by a team of leading specialists, yet suitable for novice and more experienced gardener alike, the series considers modern uses of the plants, including refreshing ideas for combining them with other garden or greenhouse plants. This should appeal to the more general gardener who, unlike the specialist, does not want to devote a large part of the garden to a particular plant. Many of the planting schemes and modern uses are beautifully illustrated in colour.

The extensive A-Z lists describe in great detail hundreds of the best varieties and species available today.

For the historically-minded, each book opens with a brief history of the subject up to the present day and, as appropriate, looks at the developments by plant breeders.

The books cover all you need to know about growing and propagating. The former embraces such aspects as suitable sites and soils, planting methods, all-year-round care and how to combat pests, diseases and disorders.

Propagation includes raising plants from seeds and by vegetative means, as appropriate.

For each subject there is a society (sometimes more), full details of which round off each book.

The plants that make up this series are very popular and examples can be found in many gardens. However, it is hoped that these books will encourage gardeners to try some of the better, or perhaps more unusual, varieties; ensure some stunning plant associations; and result in the plants being grown well.

Alan Toogood

CHAPTER ONE

PAST AND PRESENT

Camellias in real life are not the consumptive female Marguerite Gautier, La Dame aux Camélias of Dumas' novel. These mainly lime-hating plants are as long lived as *Camellia japonica* 'Alba Plena' which Captain Connor of the ss *Carnatic* brought from China in 1792 and which Marguerite loved; as shamelessly robust as the massive American 'Drama Girl'; as minuscule and charming as 'Bokuhan' from Japan; as elegant as 'Lily Pons'; as irresistible as 'Scentuous'! They are as hardy as the bay laurel and if they cannot find the leafy acid (lime-free) woodland soil and shade of their oriental homes, they will grow and flower obligingly in pots filled with acid compost.

Camellias revel in the damp air of Cornwall but they also flourish in Edinburgh and Belfast, where the International Camellia Society sponsors trials. They do well in St James's Park and Regent's Park in London; they could fully displace the sooty Victorian aucubas and privet of London's public gardens and light up its shady basements.

Camellias are international, versed in the languages of the Orient, of Brittany, the Riviera, the USA, Spain and Portugal, and are especially at home in Australasia. They are ancient yet progressive, evergreen and beautiful.

ORIGINS AND HISTORY

The origin of the generic name *Camellia* with its two pronunciations, camellia and kamelia, epitomizes the change in botanical nomenclature made by Linnaeus (1707–78). Latin was, in his day and after, the language of science and the bridge between cultures and countries. The English botanist, John Stackhouse, could, for instance, read, write, and speak Latin as fluently as his native language as recently as 1830. The Moravian missionary Joseph Kamel (1661–1706), who died a year before Linnaeus was born, could probably not have spoken a word of English but, through the universality of Latin, he could write to the eminent English botanist, John Ray, and send him drawings and descriptions of plants from Manila. There is only one camellia native to high altitudes in the Philippines, and Kamel probably never saw it or any other camellia in his life.

Linnaeus himself was a Swede, Carl Linné, but his name was latinized to Carolus Linnaeus and has remained so. He recognized that botanists were trying to compress into a considerable sentence a name for a plant which purported to describe it in some detail and he set to work to develop what is called the binomial system which gives each plant a generic name identifying it with its close relatives, and a specific name which might be descriptive or commemorative, or originant. In this case he changed phraseology such as '*Frutex Cheusanensis floribus Theae ex albo carneus fructu unicapsulari capsula trifida*' to '*Camellia japonica*'. He retained the name *Thea sinensis* for the tea plant and the controversy over this continued until the Botanical Congress of 1935 placed it under the name *Camellia*.

Linnaeus, through John Ray's correspondence with Georgius Josephus Camelus, whom he referred to as 'Father Camelli', assumed that the Jesuit priest was English and gave his name, as *Camellia*, to this important genus of trees and shrubs, the subject of this book. Buried far away from his native Germany, Father Kamel sleeps, unaware of such a great and lasting memorial.

Ornamental camellias are linked, historically and botanically with tea, trade and China. The links were forged by the ships' captains, inspectors, and surgeons of the Portuguese, Dutch and English East India Companies in that order.

To begin with they sent home dried specimens of camellia species which excited the interest of botanists, who then urged them to ship living plants. This they did in the 18th century. We do not know when the first arrived but about 1739 a camellia flower made its first public appearance in England in a picture of a pheasant painted by George Edwards. We also know that the flower was in one of the range of greenhouses of 'The Noble and Curious Lord Petre' at Thorndon Hall in Essex and, about the same time, a 'healthy tea-tree' was seen in the orangery of one of the directors of the East India Company.

A surgeon of that company, James Cunningham, stimulated the desire to import ornamental camellias by employing one Dr Bun-Ko to make no less than 1,464 coloured drawings of Chinese plants which, through their acquisition by Sir Hans Sloane, one of the greatest physicians and botanists of the 18th Century, became one of the foundation accessions of the British Museum of Natural History.

FIRST INTRODUCTIONS

To Captain Connor of the English East India Company's ss *Carnatic* must go the credit for bringing safely home to Britain the first named ornamental camellia, the double white *C. japonica* 'Alba Plena' and the mottled semi-double 'Variegata'. These were quickly followed by 'Rubra Plena' in 1794, 'Incarnata', 'Carnea', 'Variabilis' and 'Fimbriata' in 1816 and then 'Paeoni-flora'. Several of these are still grown in Britain today and large trees of some, introduced by the early settlers, remain

in Australia and New Zealand.

From these varieties, seedlings were raised and by 1825 Alfred Chandler of Vauxhall issued a catalogue including, among his own varieties, *C. japonica* 'Elegans', a camellia widely grown today and still giving rise to viable 'sports' in the USA.

The first boom in camellia growing followed, with large collections being accumulated, described and illustrated by the Abbé Berlese in France, Samuel Curtis in England and the Verschaffelts, father and son, in Belgium.

For some obscure reason camellias went out of fashion, almost the world over, about 1870.

TEA

One camellia which did not go out of fashion is *C. sinensis*, the Chinese source of tea.

Tea ranks second to water in the world's beverages and dates back to the reign of the Chinese emperor Shen Lung in the 28th century BC. By the time of the 'Cha' ching or 'Tea Classic', written by Lu Yu in the 8th century AD, during the T'ang dynasty, tea had become the national drink.

For a relatively short time during the Mongol occupation from 1280 to 1380 AD tea went out of fashion. Genghis Khan preferred mare's milk or rice wine. Marco Polo, who learned five languages, and travelled widely on behalf of Kublai Khan during his 18 years in China, mentioned rhubarb, ginger, galingale, lavender, pears, cinnamon, wheat, rice but not tea plants unless his 'small bushes, not unlike laurels, with little white flowers in Kaindu' were of *C. sinensis*.

After the Mongols, the native Ming Dynasty restored tea to its prime status and, before the dynasty's end in 1644, the tea trade with Europe had begun. As soon as tea became fashionable in England it was taxed at eight pence a gallon. This was in 1660. On 28th September of that year Pepys recorded in his famous diary his first taste of 'tee (a China drink)'.

The East India Company discouraged the production of tea in India and, in fact, the Chinese tea plant does not thrive in India and it is the sub-species, *C. s. assamica*, which makes up the colossal quantity of tea harvested outside China: 453,000,000 kg a year in India, 172,000,000 kg in Sri Lanka, a similar quantity in Africa and a little in Australia and New Zealand. China now produces about 172,000,000 kg of tea a year.

Two other economic products are derived from camellias. Oil is pressed from the seeds of *C. japonica* in Japan, from selected forms of *C. oleifera* and other species, such as *C. forrestii*, in China and from *C. reticulata* in Australia. It is used for cooking and in cosmetics. High quality charcoal is also made from camellia trees.

REVIVAL OF CAMELLIA CULTIVATION

Two great plant collectors, E. H. ('Chinese') Wilson and George Forrest were the founders of the current boom in camellia growing. George Forrest made seven expeditions to Western China between 1910 and 1932, when he died at Tengyueh in Yunnan.

One of his expeditions was sponsored by J. C. Williams of Caerhays Castle in Cornwall. To him Forrest sent seeds of *C. saluenensis*. This is not a particularly hardy camellia but it has the power to instil hardiness in hybrids of which it is the seed parent even when the pollen parent is a relatively tender camellia such as *C. reticulata*.

C. saluenensis has narrower leaves than those of *C. japonica*, single flowers in great profusion up to 7 cm (2¾ in) in diameter on a bush growing up to 5 m (16½ ft) wide and tall. The colour of the flowers varies from white to rose to magenta-pink. In severe winters it is sometimes defoliated. It uses sunshine with great efficiency, so that whereas *japonica* camellias will grow in Scotland, but either fail to flower or produce deformed flowers, the hybrids between *C. saluenensis* and *C. japonica* will withstand the winter and flower freely at least as far north as Perth, where many of them are on trial.

J. C. Williams was a man of enormous energy and prescience, gardening on a great scale in a climate which then enabled camellias to seed freely. When *C. saluenensis* flowered he crossed it with *C. japonica* and planted the hillside west of the castle with the seedlings. The first one, which received the highest awards of the Royal Horticultural Society, was named 'J. C. Williams' and many others, known as *C. × williamsii* hybrids, followed: 'Mary Christian'

'*Capt. Rawes' ss Warren Hastings in which he brought his* reticulata *namesake in 1820 from Canton (courtesy India Office library).*

named after his wife, 'Charles Michael', 'Beatrice Michael', 'Mary Larcom', 'St Ewe', 'Rosemary Williams', 'Mary Jobson' and 'Muskoka' and finally, by using 'Akashi-gata' ('Lady Clare') as the pollen parent, two large paeony flowers were raised, 'Caerhays' and 'George Blandford', of which the latter is by far the better.

Another great gardener, Col. Stephenson Clarke of Borde Hill in Sussex, England, had a share of Forrest's seeds and he crossed *C. saluenensis*, a particularly good form, with *C. japonica* 'Masayoshi' ('Donckelaeri') and raised *C. × williamsii* 'Donation', probably the world's most popular camellia. Further progress in the × *williamsii* hybrids emerges in Chapter 3.

J. C. Williams received from Wilson seeds of *C. cuspidata*, which Wilson incorrectly rated the hardiest of all camellias. The hardiness is about on a par with that of *C. saluenensis* with which species J. C. Williams promptly crossed it. 'Cornish Snow' is the principal result, 'Winton' a lesser one. In my opinion 'Cornish Snow' is the best landscape white camellia.

Miss Carlyon of Tregrehan, not far from Caerhays, crossed *C. cuspidata* with *C. japonica* 'Rosea Simplex' and named the seedling 'Cornish Spring', but did not follow up this very valuable initiative. An American hybrid is 'Spring Festival': very, very hardy, late, and closely upright-growing with small formal double pink flowers.

Using pollen of *C. reticulata* on *C. saluenensis* a few very hardy hybrids have been raised, closely resembling × *williamsii* hybrids. 'Inspiration', 'Dr Louis Pollizzi' and 'Free Style' are examples.

Similarly from *C. reticulata* crossed with *C. sasanqua*, very hardy winter-flowering fragrant hybrids have been raised in America. Their scent in a greenhouse is almost too strong. *C. sasanqua* is the small-leaved autumn- or winter-flowering species from Japan of which the cultivars run into hundreds. They tolerate a neutral or slightly alkaline soil, need sun and, flowering at a frosty time of year, require in Britain a sheltered place, on a wall or in a greenhouse or a place in central London, where the temperature is higher.

The vast majority of cultivated camellias originated from *C. japonica*, a large and beautiful single red camellia native to Japan. Foliage and flowers of the varieties bred from it vary widely from, for instance, the broad bold leaves and formal flowers of 'Souvenir de Bahuaud Litou' to the small leaves and miniature red and white anemone flowers of 'Bokuhan'. The mountain forms known as *rusticana* are not so hardy – they lie under a winter duvet of 9 m (30 ft) of snow! *C. reticulata* was represented for many years outside China by a large semi-double named 'Capt Rawes', after the captain of the East India Company's ship *Warren Hastings*, on which he brought a plant from Canton in 1820.

John Damper Parkes brought an almost identical plant in 1824. It is thought that one of these is fertile, one sterile. Later, Robert Fortune, at mid-century, introduced a double red *reticulata* camellia variously named *C. r.*

'Flore Pleno', 'Robert Fortune' and 'Pagoda' but now known to be 'Song-zilin' from Yunnan.

From 1949 onwards many ancient *reticulata* camellias have been introduced from Yunnan to the USA and New Zealand, and thence worldwide. They were, in fact, listed in a Chinese book of the eleventh century AD, the *Cha-Hua-Pua* by P. Chao. From a nurseryman's point-of-view they are beautiful, but dangerous as carriers of leaf-mottle virus. Virus is not seed-borne so that innumerable healthy hybrids are available with flowers ranging up to 18 cm (7 in) in diameter. They can be grown outdoors in Britain only in Cornwall, the Channel Islands, Southern Ireland and inner London.

It was not until 1923 that the wild single form of *C. reticulata* was recognized among the camellias collected by George Forrest. Bushes of various forms of this fine camellia have reached 9 m (30 ft) high at Caerhays and Trewithen in Cornwall. Of some 200 remaining species of camellia about eight deserve mention here. *C. c. tsaii* and *taliensis* bear white flowers in winter in Cornwall and are being used to raise interesting hybrids in New Zealand.

C. lutchuensis is by far the favourite source of scented hybrids. It is a small tree, with small white flowers, growing on Okinawa and other Japanese islands.

C. granthamiana from Hong Kong has distinctive foliage and large romneya-like, white flowers opening from dead-looking papery buds. It is possibly hardy in Cornwall and a good greenhouse plant elsewhere.

C. fraterna with small scented flowers is yielding some useful hybrids in the USA and the Antipodes. *C. pitardii* also, with a flower nearer to *C. reticulata*.

Finally *C. chrysantha* and *C. euphlebia*, two yellow-flowered camellias available in the west. The first has flowered in the USA, Japan and Australia and, already, a vast amount of use has been made of the pollen but the quickly achieved yellow, apricot and orange camellias which were heralded so liberally, have not yet emerged.

C. chrysantha is in a much more primitive group than *C. japonica*. *C. luteoflora*, miniature in flower, only 1–1.8 cm (⅜–¾ in) in diameter, but more closely related, gives, in theory, more hope of successful yellow hybrids.

CHAPTER TWO

PLANTING IDEAS

For two reasons this chapter is difficult to write. First, Cornwall, with its favourable climate, ought to demonstrate the best plant associations, but it does not, because the large gardens where they should be visible do not have them at ground level but only at *Magnolia mollicomata*-cum-camellia level, far beyond the reach of the average gardener. Secondly, in a humid maritime climate almost everything in a small garden can luxuriate in close proximity. Close to the Helford river bushes of × *williamsii* camellias alternate with bushes of *Erica lusitanica*; the scent is delicious. Inland, the camellias would require a more shaded position than the heathers.

Shade is the inland equivalent of, or dispenser of, humidity. A high coniferous canopy also radiates warmth.

I propose to divide the chapter into five sections:
1. Trees and shrubs for shelter.
2. Trees to give to a planting contrasting height and beneficial shade.
3. Shrubs to provide interest concurrently and, also, later in the year when camellia flowers are over.
4. Herbaceous and bulbous plants enjoying the same conditions as camellias.
5. Companions for camellias in greenhouses.

1. TREES AND SHRUBS FOR SHELTER

This heading is not a confession of weakness! Camellias will withstand as much ordinary wind as any evergreen. But few evergreens will survive unharmed the windchill from only a few degrees of frost intensified by the high velocity of an east wind, circumstances fairly frequent in late winter during the 1980s in southern Britain. Desiccation with wind-frost is a greater enemy than a harder frost in calm air. So, for a large garden, wind should be filtered through trees to reduce its velocity. For this purpose *Pinus radiata* used to be planted because it is a fast grower and dense while growing. Ordinary Scots pine, *Pinus sylvestris*, is in many respects preferable for it grows well almost everywhere in Britain. *Pinus nigra*, the Austrian pine, or its subspe-

cies *P. n. maritima*, the Corsican pine, are quick growing and wind resistant, especially the Corsican. The roots of young pine trees are shallow. Eventually any of these will become a canopy above a bare trunk and thus necessitate the planting of evergreen shrubs between the trees, to protect the garden. Bamboos are, or were, widely used for this purpose and work well until they flower and die, when there is an interval of two or three years before seedlings take over. However, never plant a *Sasa* but use *Arundinaria japonica* or other non-running, clump-forming species. The evergreen which is widely used instead is *Elaeagnus macrophylla*. This, or *E. pungens*, will withstand a lot of wind and, when mature, produce inconspicuous sweetly scented flowers in autumn but they can both be browned by a wind-frost. *Rhododendron ponticum* can be used, but it seeds around and *R.* 'Fastuosum Flore Plena' will do a better job and be more attractive.

The most magnificent wind-break for a large garden is the Wellingtonia, *Sequoiadendron giganteum*, which stays furnished nearly down to ground level. It is one of the few trees which survived the great storm in October 1987 in the south-east of England.

Looking at shelter for smaller gardens, it is necessary to make one qualifying statement. Almost any evergreen, and certainly conifers, however fastigiate their tops, limiting their space re-

Opposite: *The late-flowering* × williamsii *'Lady's Maid' associating with an evergreen azalea.*

quirements above ground to say 0.75 m (2½ ft) wide, will have a shallow spread of roots in diameter more like the height of the tree. Thus, a wind-filter of *Chamaecyparis lawsoniana* 'Wisselii' now about 6 m (20 ft) high and 1.5 m (5 ft) spread has a shallow root system for some 3 m (10 ft) on each side of the trunk. Any camellia planted within this area will be robbed by the conifer.

The choice of closely upright conifers for small gardens is wide, including the cultivars of *Chamaecyparis lawsoniana* named 'Columnaris', 'Allumii', 'Fraseri', 'Hillieri' and 'Kilmacurragh'.

The Leyland cypress, × *Cupressocyparis leylandii*, has taken a leading and versatile role in providing shelter and can reach 21 m (70 ft) high very quickly or be clipped regularly to as little as 1.2 m (4 ft) high.

It is a general rule that a conifer planted young at 45 cm (1½ ft) high, with a young root system, will outstrip a larger plant 1–1.5 m (3¼–5 ft) high with a restricted root-ball.

If a deciduous tree is required to provide some shelter and shade on the boundary of a large garden, *Nothofagus obliqua* is very quick-growing but its head of foliage is comparatively thin, a wind-filter rather than a wind-stopper.

Beech is a shallow-rooted robber; sycamore Alan Mitchell rightly called an 'ecological disaster'! More on that later!

My line of outer shelter from the great winds of Cornwall is of *Tilia × euchlora*, a stout lime tree which does not have a sticky lot of aphis and which branches and renews itself well and, as it flowers, feeds the bees.

2. TREES TO GIVE HEIGHT AND CONTRAST

Let us start with the giant magnolias of southern counties: *M. campbellii* and its forms *M. c.* 'Alba' and *M. c. mollicomata*, *M. c.* 'Charles Raffill', *M. c.* 'Lanarth', *M.* 'Dawsoniana', *M. sargentiana robusta*, *M. sprengeri*, *M. × veitchii*, *M.* 'Caerhays Belle', and others. These are nearly all big trees in terms of height, spread of roots and branches, requiring on their own up to 0.1 hectare (¼ acre) each if allowed to grow unimpeded to full spread in maturity as they should be. Their massive flowers are all shades of pink and purple, except the white *M. campbellii* 'Alba'. *M. c.* 'Lanarth', a smaller tree, can be a livid shade of magenta-purple.

Most of these require between ten to eighteen years before flowering. Two new ones from New Zealand raised by Felix Jury, 'Iolanthe', near in colour and size to *M. c. mollicomata*, and 'Mark Jury' nearer to 'Lanarth', flower soon after planting.

All of these magnolias root very near the surface of the ground, in fact *M. c. mollicomata* is liable to thrust 'knees' through the grass if planted near a lawn and they must not be damaged. Therefore, any association with camellias has to be worked out beforehand and planted while the magnolia is young.

I have the good fortune, while writing in early spring, to be able to look out of the window at a couple of bushes of *Camellia* 'Cornish Snow' with a combined spread of 6 m (20 ft) and height of 3 m (10 ft) in full white flower, backed by a young tree of *Magnolia campbellii mollicomata* almost at its best in flower, with a spread of 10.6 m (35 ft) and a little more in height. The camellias were planted 4.5 m (15 ft) from the stem of the young magnolia some twenty years ago. To complete the picture there is in front of the 'Cornish Snow' a bush of the fastigiate camellia hybrid 'Spring Festival' for later flowering. Behind the group is an enormous holly, some 9 m (30 ft) wide and 12 m (40 ft) high, framing the magnolia flowers against an opaque background.

□ THE SMALLER MAGNOLIAS

To provide height among camellias in smaller gardens there is a range of white magnolias which will make small trees. They are often seen as bushes branched to ground level which inhibits close association with other shrubs. I prefer to see them as small trees. The same rule holds good – plant while young.

Magnolias used to be sold from open ground, with tender roots exposed, and were easily damaged. They took a long time to get established. They can now be bought in containers and, provided a plant is bought young and is not root bound, it will grow away and can easily be trained into a small tree with a trunk. As the leading shoot of a plant – 60 cm (2 ft) high when planted – grows upwards, side branches will grow out at right angles to the main stem. To start with, these are tipped to prevent any competition with the leader. When the main stem has become stout enough to stand on its own, the side shoots are progressively cut off during the summer close to the trunk up to a height of, say, 1.5 m (5 ft). This young tree will then grow a head of both upright and lateral branches and would in the old days have been called a half-standard. This does not apply to *M. stellata*, which remains shrubby, nor to the various forms of *M. × soulangeana*, *M. sieboldii* or *M. × watsonii*, all of which prefer to grow multi-stemmed. It applies to the white-flowered magnolias: *M. kobus* and *M. k. borealis*, *M. salicifolia*, *M. sinensis*, *M. × highdownensis*, *M. × proctoriana*, *M.* 'Kewensis', *M.* 'Merrill' *M.* 'Leonard Messel' and *M. wilsonii*. Of these *M. sinensis*, *M. × highdownensis*, and *M. wilsonii* are the more difficult to train into standard trees. *M. × proctoriana* is a smaller grower too and 'Leonard Messel' has pink flowers.

Shallow-rooted trees try to shield their roots, which means that the lower branches incline towards the ground. In terms of plant association, this enables the gardener to plan an association of greater and lesser plants, which may contain an element of contrast or even surprise, but he may also have to be prepared later to do some cutting out, in this case perhaps a whole branch of a magnolia. This should be done during the latter half of the growing season.

The magnolias listed above vary in strength and it is not wise to specify ultimate dimensions but a tree of *M. loebneri* will serve as an example. At a height of 7.5 m (25 ft), the spread of a half standard tree is 9 m (30 ft). In this case grape hyacinths (muscari) are planted between the lawn grass and the trunk: they will be over before the tree

The popular early, dependable, × williamsii *hybrid 'St Ewe' in a pleasant plant association.*

One of two great plants of C. reticulata *'Capt. Rawes', superbly trained on the rear wall of Joseph Paxton's greenhouse at Chatsworth, home of the Duke of Devonshire in Derbyshire.*

is in leaf.

Camellia × *williamsii* 'Freedom Bell' has a red colour difficult to place among a family of pink × *williamsii* hybrids. Placed on its own in front of a tree of *Magnolia* 'Merrill', its flowering overlaps that of the magnolia which pervades it with apple-blossom fragrance and, to complete a picture with contrasting foliage, a plant of the low shrub *Xanthorhiza simplicissima*, the yellow root, with deeply toothed pinnate leaves, grows in front of the camellia.

Mahonias also provide contrasting pinnate foliage alongside. Their yellow flowers are over before the camellia blooms and their purple fruits harmonize. The most bushy is 'Buckland', the best of the taller ones is 'Lionel Fortescue'.

Planting a garden is largely a matter of one's own choice, subject to the compatibility of the plants chosen. The original planting of camellias in Regent's Park, London has a historical significance – it demonstrated that camellias could be grown in London. In fact London has a winter-temperature advantage largely unexploited. But these camellias had no companion plants. A later planting was mixed.

□ OTHER COMPANION TREES

Camellias are, by nature, woodland shrubs or small trees requiring an acid, leafy soil and, generally, some shade.

It is, therefore, possible to name small trees compatible with camellias not only in these respects but also in what may be termed 'atmosphere'. To illustrate that, I would regard a la-burnum as incompatible with a camellia. At the other end of the scale, yellow trumpet daffodils would also be disqualified!

An obvious first choice is one of the same family as the camellia, *Theaceae*, the stuartia, with horizontal branches lined with white cupped flowers on short stalks in mid-summer. The species obtainable are probably *S. pseudocamellia*, *S. koreana*, and *S. sinensis*. Stuartias should be restricted to one main trunk, for the bark and the autumn colour of the leaves are both striking. The stuartia likes full sun and in the process of enjoying it gives moderate welcome shade to the camellias with which it keeps company.

Alphabetically and culturally styrax comes next. *S. japonica* is the most common, a small graceful tree up to 7.5 m (25 ft), laden with little white bells in early summer. *S. hemsleyana* has spikes of white snowdrops in early summer and exceeds 12 m (40 ft) in height at Caerhays in Cornwall. *S. obassia* has larger leaves, spikes of white fragrant flowers, and grows to 6–9 m (20–30 ft) in height. *Halesia carolina*, the snowdrop tree, fits in here, belonging to the same family. It also grows up to 6–9 m (20–30 ft) in height, with its branches lined in late spring with white bells followed by brown, winged fruit. *Halesia monticola* is a timber tree in the USA but its form *H. m. rosea* is, in Britain, a slender grower, a small tree. Sticking to the same family, *Pterostyrax hispida* comes next, having once been a halesia. It is a lighter, late shrub or small tree with soft wood and hanging panicles of small white flowers in summer. On a sunny day their fragrance is noticeable.

With fragrance the objective, plus a complete contrast in foliage, *Elaeagnus multiflora* may be admitted. It can with care be trained with a single stem to make a small tree 3–4.5 m (10–15 ft) high and wide, with grey leaves and abundant pale creamy-yellow tubular flowers in spring and summer, spreading a delightful cinnamon scent all around. In Asia and the USA it fruits freely but not in Britain.

Parrotiopsis jacquemontiana is not a spectacular small tree but it has the right atmosphere to accompany camellias. The leaves are hazel-like, the flowers surrounded by white petaloid 'bracts', like little bottle-brushes.

Birches may be safe consorts on richer soils but on the thinner soils of the Bagshot sand formation, or anywhere liable to drought, they are robbers to be excluded from the company of camellias. So are maples.

The flowering dogwoods are readily admissible. In Cornwall and Southern Ireland *Cornus capitata* makes a tree with pale yellow, almost white 'flowers' and strawberry-like fruits. Elsewhere it is tender. The safer associate is *Cornus kousa* which holds out tiers of innumerable white bracts in late spring and early summer and has red autumn leaf colour. *C. k. chinensis* has larger 'flowers' and a more upright habit.

The arbutus belong to the heather family and in association with camellias supply the contrasting red colour of their bark and spikes of bell-shaped flowers.

Liquidambar styraciflua, a larger tree than those mentioned so far, has maple-like leaves and brilliant autumn colour.

Evergreen shrubs like the eucryphias, which are tree-like and demand a shaded root-run, fit in here. They extend the flowering season to late summer but they are regarded as reliably hardy only in the southern counties of Britain. The four-petalled white flowers have conspicuously beautiful stamens. *E. × nymansensis* 'Nymansay' is the most popular, reaching 12 m (40 ft) or more in height. *E. cordifolia* grows over 16 m (53 ft) high in Cornwall but generally is more tender than 'Nymansay'.

Embothriums are further examples of shrubs and small trees, mostly of South American origin, which like their roots in the cool and their heads in the sun. Their contrasting foliage and upright habit fit well with camellias and most of their flowering follows on. In height they nearly equal *Eucryphia × nymansensis* 'Nymansay' but they have a longer flowering period, from mid-spring to early summer in the case of the broad-leaved suckering form found in Cornwall. The narrower, small lanceolate-leaved form is hardier. The yellow and white varieties have not yet been widely distributed.

Finally in this category, a small tree or sometimes a shrub, *Telopea truncata*, from the high altitudes of Tasmania. It has much pendant branching with long narrow dark evergreen leaves and terminal clusters of deep crimson chrysanthemum-like flowers in early summer. It needs the same conditions as embothrium – head in the sun, feet in the shade, acid leafy soil and shelter. A much more spectacular bushy teleopea is *T. oreades* or its form *mongaensis* but this is less hardy.

3. SHRUBS TO ASSOCIATE WITH CAMELLIAS

There is practically nothing in the literature or in illustrations which deals with the pros and cons of the association of other shrubs with the evergreen weight of camellia foliage.

One might be a purist and dictate no association and, indeed, there are situations where this may be correct. In a formal garden or a formal corner in a town garden where a camellia is in an urn or stone trough or other container, as a part of the composition primarily for the quality of its foliage, the camellia should be self-sufficient and need no company. Equally so as a hedge.

There are two principal places which other shrubs may occupy in association with camellias. The first is in interplanting, which requires that the shrub will share the camellias' liking for acid soil and some shade, and the second is the fringe of a camellia planting where shrubs which prefer more sun can be allowed to spread with it.

One could write the word rhododendron and leave it at that! Indeed if one wants to bring contemporaneous blue into a camellia planting the choice must fall on the rhododendrons 'Saint Tudy', 'Blue Diamond', 'Belle of Tremeer' or others. At ground level *Brunnera macrophylla* and muscari will

supply it. If scent is wanted a bush of one of the *Rhododendron* × *loderi* hybrids will add it and the foliage does not quarrel with that of camellias. It will be essential to watch the spacing; the 'Loderi' hybrids make big dominant bushes. These and most of the larger-leaved rhododendron species appreciate the half-shade which suits camellias and, certainly, they have the same soil requirements.

Let us look at other shrubs which will happily share the soil and part shade with camellias but also accentuate the value of camellia foliage by contrast.

Contrary to an earlier comment adverse to yellow, the first shrub is *Stachyurus praecox*, upright growing to 2m (6ft) or more in a half-shaded position. The leaves are hazel-like and the flowers profusely borne on soft creamy-yellow catkins early in spring. The timorous would plant it next to the camellia 'Jury's yellow', or a good white camellia, the adventurous near *C.* 'Bob Hope'! It is too characterful a shrub to leave out.

Playing safe, the sarcococcas contribute widespread scent in mid-winter, from wispy white flowers in the axils of lanceolate evergreen leaves. *S. ruscifolia* has red berries and grows quite gracefully to 1.2m (4ft) high. *S. confusa* is similar, perhaps a little taller, but with black fruits, and *S. hookeriana digyna* is dwarf, later in flower and has black berries on a compact bushy plant. It is a front-line plant. All are fit for deep shade.

Around the corner from my *Magnolia mollicomata* and *Camellia* 'Cornish

Snow' the ground slopes from the great holly to the drive. Here a clump of *C.* × *williamsiii* 'Donation' makes a background, *C.* × *w.* 'Bow Bells', flowering earlier, is in front of it. Full in front of the holly is a magnificent bush of *C. reticulata* 'Eden Roc', upright and bold, with *Azalea* 'Redwing' below it, behind a wide-spreading, ground-hugging *C. japonica* 'Taroan' with pale pink flowers and dark foliage. Alongside this is a large clump of *Philesia magellanica*. The philesia, which is 1 m (3 ft) high with narrow short dark leaves, should have many rose-crimson, bell-shaped flowers in late summer but there were two mistakes in the planting: the philesia is not in deep enough shade to make it flower and it should be where the camellia 'Taroan' is; and the sun-proof azalea needs more sun to enhance the contrasts in the group.

Two separated clumps of *Danae racemosa*, the Alexandrian laurel, are planted alongside, with the graceful growth, longer lanceolate paler green leaves, and occasional red berries, arching in front of a low bush of *Camellia japonica* 'Bokuhan' which opens its small red and white anemone flowers in mid-winter in front of the holly. Herbaceous plants grow behind the danae on higher but still shaded ground: snakes'-head fritillaries, Solomon's seal and *Maianthemum racemosum* (*Smilacina racemosa*).

From the danae, evergreen azaleas line the old drive forming a colourful border in front of × *williamsii* camellias. 'Kirin', 'Hino Crimson', 'Pekoe', 'White Lady', 'Vuyk's 'Rosy Red', 'Lady Ivor

Churchill', harmonize with the camellias; and beyond the 'White Lady' the blazing colour of 'Ward's Ruby', the best, if not the only sun-proof red azalea, finishes the planting next to a bay tree.

Kalmias are becoming more readily available through the breeding of new varieties in the USA and the use of micropropagation. *Kalmia angustifolia* is a low small-leaved species a bit above 1 m (3 ft) high with plentiful deep pink flowers, readily produced in early summer. There is a white form. It is the varieties of *K. latifolia* with larger leaves and heads of cup-shaped flowers, which resemble wedding cake icing decorations, that are more available in variety. They do not flower freely when young but the beautiful flowers are worth waiting for.

An upright evergreen, *Crinodendron hookeranum*, with crimson bells hanging in late spring amongst lanceolate leaves, loves the same conditions as camellias. It is hardy only in the south of Britain. Its white companion, *C. patagua*, is not even that.

With the same climatic limits as the crimson crinodendron, the evergreen *Itea ilicifolia* offers an eye-catching contrast with 30 cm (1 ft) green catkins hanging over brilliant evergreen holly-like leaves in late summer. Where suited it will grow 2–3 m (6½–10 ft) high and wide.

Two gaultherias, *G. hookeri* and *G. forrestii*, with oval evergreen leaves, white urn-shaped flowers and blue berries, mix well with camellias in part shade, growing up to 1.5 m (5 ft) high.

'*Joan Trehane*', *a fine rose form double upright late* × williamsii, *liking some shade.*

Avoid *G. shallon*, which suckers madly and is fit only for a bold lawn clump or a pheasant covert.

Leucothoe fontanesiana has the same 'atmosphere' as the gaultherias, a similar arching evergreen, but with narrower leaves and innumerable racemes of white urn-shaped flowers in late spring. It grows up to 2 m (6 ft) high and wide. There is a variegated form 'Rainbow' with much pink on its leaves.

A surprising evergreen, from high damp forests in Chile, is *Desfontainea spinosa* which looks just like a bushy holly until it bursts out with scarlet and yellow slim bells in late summer and autumn. In favourable conditions with damp air it is hardy and grows up to 3 m (10 ft) high, and equally wide, and always attracts attention.

Moving towards the edge of a camellia planting, the pieris have proliferated in recent years more rapidly than almost any other evergreen shrub. They rejoice in even more peat than camellias and will thrive in part shade, or full sun where the air is moist. The hardiest and a good clean white with erect spikes of urn-shaped flowers in spring is *P. floribunda*, a noticeable shrub in Britain in the Lake District. Next comes *P. taiwanensis*, also up to 2 m (6 ft) in height, but with drooping racemes of white flowers. The green bracts somehow offset the white to give the whole shrub a greeny-white appearance.

The most tender is *Pieris formosa forrestii*, a much stiffer taller shrub up to 5.5 m (18 ft) high with large leaves and stiffer spikes of white flowers. The 'Wakehurst' form is the best in general trade, with vivid red young leaves and a robust look about it but, alas, the young foliage can be burnt back by a spring frost and in a very severe winter the whole bush can be cut to the ground. It will normally regenerate quickly.

Between these comes a rapidly increasing number of forms of *Pieris japonica*, all evergreens with clustering racemes of lily-of-the-valley-like flowers, white not only on the species but also on many of the forms available, but now augmented by many pink and crimson varieties. All are good, well-clothed evergreens liable to lose their red young shoots in a late spring frost but quickly making good the damage.

When one gardener has eighty-four different cultivars on trial who shall say which are the most desirable? For coloured spring foliage 'Firecrest', 'Flame of the Forest', 'Mountain Fire' and 'Valley Fire' are good. For white flowers 'White Cascade' excels. 'Wada's Pink' with very soft pink flowers was the first coloured pieris to arrive; a demure plant. 'Flamingo' has long strings of carmine flowers starting very early in late winter. *P. j.* 'Variegata' has the normal growth of the species but the leaves are variegated with yellow and white. There are dwarf forms: 'Bisbee Dwarf', small enough for a rock garden; 'Little Heath', for edging, along with its distinctive variegated form. Another low growing pieris is 'Purity' which grows thickly – no more than 1 m (3 ft) high but a little wider with green leaves and spikes of white flowers. It resembles *P. floribunda* more than *P. japonica*.

A group of shrubs for scent, a treasured possession remarked by every visitor to the garden. First the skimmias. The male plants are the most fragrant, the females in the trade have red berries like holly, and one, *S. reevesiana*, is dwarf, only 60 cm (2 ft) high, and bisexual, a charming shrub, but remember it will be brilliant red when the camellias are in flower. Plant it alongside *Camellia japonica* 'Lily Pons' for all round quality. Skimmias like half shade. A planting of *S. japonica* 'Rubella' (male) with *S. j.* 'Nymans' (female) combines all these virtues. Continuing the pursuit of scent, two clethras get away from the evergreens and from spring into the late summer. Reminiscent of the herbaceous cimicifugas, *Clethra alnifolia* and *C. tomentosa* and, possibly, *C. fargesii*, grow up to 3 m (10 ft) high, suckering slightly. The scent of the spikes of white flowers spreads agreeably.

Zenobia pulverulenta is a short glaucous evergreen with a scruffy look if the flowered stems are not removed. The white, bell-shaped flowers spread scent in mid-summer. It is a front-row plant 1–2 m (3¼–6½ ft) high.

The enkianthus fit well as front line shrubs in sun with the same soil requirements as camellias. They are deciduous with tiered branching, laden with pink, white or buff bells, growing from 1.5 m (5 ft) for *E. cernuus rubens*, which has brilliant autumn colour, to double that height or more for *E. chinensis*.

There is a quartet of deciduous azaleas, which no suitable garden should be without on the fringe of a planting of camellias. Their fragrance is enchanting and they range from the 1 m

(3 ft) high *Rhododendron atlanticum*, with pink and white honeysuckle-like flowers, to the richer pink, yellow and white flower trusses of *R. occidentale* in summer on spreading bushes as much as 3 m (10 ft) high. In between are *R. canadense*, nearer to *R. atlanticum* in height and time but with darker flowers, and *R. viscosum*, the swamp honeysuckle, 2 m (6 ft) or more high, 'exquisitely fragrant' in full summer.

4. HERBACEOUS AND BULBOUS PLANTS ENJOYING THE SAME CONDITIONS AS CAMELLIAS

There are some clear favourites here! What better setting for *Cardiocrinum giganteum* (*Lilium giganteum*) than a clearing among *japonica* camellias? Those majestic spikes standing 2–3 m (6½–10 ft) high with broad heart-shaped leaves and downward-inclined white trumpets will fill such a clearing with dignity and fragrance in summer. The bulbs like the same soil, plenty of peat or leaf-mould or even some old manure. The classic advice was to plant where one's favourite hunter was buried!

PLANTING DEPTH

The bulbs should only just be covered and are usually offered in three sizes for succession as the bulb which has flowered breaks up into offsets which take a year or two to gather strength to flower again.

There are other plants suited to the above effect, *Lobelia cardinalis* for one. Like *L. vedrarienses*, purple, the old 'Queen Victoria', needs staking but cultivars 'Will Scarlett', 'Dark Crusader', 'Darkness' and, best of all, 'Brightness', do not and they will stand light shade. They will make their mark alone against camellia foliage, but the taller white cimifugas can be planted behind if greater complexity is desired. Lobelias are easily increased by prising rosettes from a clump in late spring and potting them up for later planting.

At the other end of the scale come my personal garden favourites, two or three dogs' tooth violets or erythroniums, not the ephemeral European ones but the taller, more robust ones from Oregon. In flower early or mid-spring *Erythronium revolutum johnsonii* is without peer. The colour and set of the flowers have an air of quality hallmarked by the marbled leaves. This tuberous plant is rare and expensive but sets seed readily and, provided it is sown absolutely as soon as the pod shows a sign of splitting, it comes up like salad onions next spring. It takes three years to flower.

Omitting the yellows, *E. tuolumnensis* and *E. t.* 'Pagoda', *E. revolutum* 'White Beauty' is less tall and graceful but a lovely flower.

The tubers are brittle and should be planted vertically in very leafy or peaty soil, in sun or shade where the air is moist, and in part shade elsewhere. The colours of leaf and flower will be enriched by sunshine.

Again, looking first at the essential quality of companionship in the growing conditions and atmosphere that camellias enjoy, the subject can be divided into close companion plants and foreground plants, fitting the plants to the amount of shared light and shade.

Taking the companion plants first, that is herbaceous plants which can happily be fitted into spaces between camellias either temporarily while growing, or permanently, the meconopsis fit the temporary category because they are not good perennials and decay unless divided every other year after flowering and even then they are brittle to handle and easily bruised and lost. *Meconopsis betonicifolia* (*M. baileyi*), the blue poppy, seeds freely. The strain known as 'Crewdson Hybrids' is supposed to have *M. grandis* in its parentage but it looks and behaves like a good form of *M. betonicifolia*. *M. betonicifolia alba* is available but, from seed, not reliably true.

Meconopsis grandis 'S 600', or 'Branklyn', and *M. g.* 'Slieve Donard' are larger, 1.2 m (4 ft) and more, leafy and set seed in the north better than in Cornwall. *M. chelidonifolia* has yellow flowers and will stand more sun and seeds freely, as does the shorter *M. villosa*.

Avoid *Meconopsis cambrica*, the Welsh poppy; nice foliage and flowers but a tenacious weed and no fit companion for a camellia.

Polygonatum, Solomon's seal, fits here with its arching stems and white and green hanging bells followed by black berries. *P. canaliculatum* is much taller, up to 1.5 m (5 ft), if the true plant is obtained!

A close relative but stiffer, more leafy and lower growing at 75 cm (2½ ft) or less, always attracts attention, and it should be labelled clearly *Maianthemum racemosum* (*Smilacina racemosa*), otherwise its pleasant scent which spreads around will prompt everyone to ask its name. It is smilacina in the trade. A companion and equally a good perennial could be, in the trade, a dentaria, named in *Index Hortensis* cardamine. For practical purposes they resemble the wild cuckoo flower and there are available *C. heptaphylla*, white, *C. pentaphyllos*, lilac, and possibly *C. kitaibelii*, white. They have rhizomes which are thick, white and toothed – hence the old name. Height varies from 30 cm (1 ft) to 38 cm (15 in). They flower in late spring in sun or shade and hold pinnate foliage until early autumn.

The toad lilies or tricyrtis species and hybrids have the oriental style and colouring designed to go with camellias. Their flowers are autumnal and with one exception their heads of trumpet-shaped flowers face upwards, in colours ranging from yellow, white or shades of light purple, and spotted.

A much bolder plant, also from Japan, and similar in its autumn impact, is *Kirengeshoma palmata*, growing up to 1 m (3¼ ft) and as much or more wide with broad sycamore-like leaves on arching stems ending in creamy yellow bells. It is a greedy plant with a large root-system but it shows up well against camellia foliage and will enjoy dense shade.

Flowering at about the same time is the willow-leaved gentian, *Gentiana asclepiadea*, filling the same space with many slender stems lined with blue trumpets. By comparison its white form is a poor thing. The species seeds freely and far, if content, and a good plant has a life of about five years before dying of fecundity.

In the same class but very different in form is *Astrantia maxima* with good broad leaves and wide-petalled, dusky pink flowers in summer. In good soil and plenty of space it suckers steadily and makes an eye-catching rounded clump needing no support. Indeed none of the plants named, or to be named here, require staking, a symbol of the unnatural, and alien to camellias.

One persicaria, (polygonum in the trade) can be admitted; autumnal *P. amplexicaule*, filling a space 1.2 m (4 ft) wide and high with spikes of crimson flowers. It seeds a little but suckers not at all. There is a dwarf form also flowering in the autumn. Avoid the giant persicarias (polygonums), *P. cuspidatum* and *P. sachalinense*, like the plague.

Some of the true geraniums fit in here, notably the mourning widow, *G. phaeum*, which makes a bold clump of buttercup-like leaves, 75 cm (2½ ft) wide and high, and loves the shade, where it can seed too freely. The flowers are black but there is a white form, a soft slate-blue form and some attractive hybrids such as 'Lily Lovell'. An equally robust geranium with more spread is *G.* 'Claridge Druce' with plenty of rich pink flowers. It is very much a giant form of *G. endressii* which is a very long-lived perennial, varying a little in the pink shades of its flowers. This hybridizes with *G. nodosum*, a shorter long-flowering magenta-pink. These, *G. sylvaticum* and its excellent varieties, and others, do well in some shade.

One of the best plant associations I have seen is of *Geranium libani* with a soft pink camellia. This is a tuberous geranium which carries its fresh new foliage through the winter and just contrives to send up its rich almost blue flowers to keep company with the flowers of, say, *Camellia × williamsii* 'Charles Colbert'. This geranium seeds moderately.

Three geraniums can become scandent among camellia foliage. One, *G. lambertii*, has nodding, bowl-shaped, pale pink flowers with crimson lines inside the petals. The other, *G. wallichianum* 'Buxton's Variety', has white-centred, bright blue flowers from summer through autumn. Both are good value and no trouble. The third, *G. procurrens*, a lively purple, is more rampageous and roots as it goes. Some gardeners laboriously trim off the foliage of hardy geraniums in the autumn. If the sight of brown stems, which are but blankets, can be borne until the spring they can then be swished off with a long-handled fork in no time at all and composted or burnt.

Contrasts do not have to be complicated to succeed. The ordinary male fern, *Dryopteris filix-mas*, with its feathery fronds is as simple and good a companion for a camellia as one could wish for. Just as Reginald Kaye made a plea for the lower basements of London to be made verdant with ferns, I would say that most London basements, with the construction of a simple rectangular bed from concrete blocks, could be embellished by a camellia. *C. × williamsii* 'Francie L' or *C. × w.* 'Elegant Beauty' trained on the wall and one or more ferns could complete a picture not to be forgotten.

The male fern is big and makes a stock almost like a tree fern but it is cheap, easy and effective. If one wants less vigour and greater refinement, plant a crested form or a lady fern, *Athyrium filix-femina*, plain or crested.

At some time, Capt. Pinwill, the original designer of my garden, planted crested ferns in one part of the garden and in that area today, nearly a century later, many of the self-sown male ferns grow crested fronds.

Many more ferns could be mentioned here but we will rest with two: the first the lovely dwarf oak fern, *Gymnocarpium dryopteris*, with its delicate spreading green fronds 23 cm (9 in) high, and, at the other end of the scale, the ostrich fern, *Matteuccia struthiopteris*, with green shuttlecocks 1 m (3¼ ft) or more high, encircling brown fruiting fronds. This fern spreads underground, erupting as much as 1–2 m (3¼–6½ ft) away, soon making a considerable patch eligible for the alcove effect.

It is a good indicator plant. As soon as the big fronds show signs of browning it is time for the hosepipe or the sprinkler to cool down the camellias.

A word of warning! The male fern is intrusive. Its fertile spores blow into every nook and cranny of walls, rock gardens and matted plants like dicentra and arabis and, unnoticed, grow. The fern can be had for nothing, the little stainless steel winkler, like a small pointed trowel, must be bought! It will be needed!

Aruncus dioicus (*A. sylvester*) and *A. d.* 'Kneiffii', all white, are up in the 1–1½ m (3¼–5 ft) class. The astilbes, in many shades of pink and red as well as white, are shorter. All have light finely cut foliage. *Filipendula purpurea*, 1.2 m (4 ft), has plainer leaves as has its taller, 2 m (6½ ft) relative, *F. rubra*, a robust invader best given an alcove of camellias all to itself. The foliage of all these summer-flowering perennials contrasts well with the evergreen mass of camellias. Reminiscent of them in flower but with broader, rhubarb-like leaves come the rodgersias, lovers of moisture exceeding the thirst of camellias but they will get by with ample peat or leafmould and no competition. The cimicifugas also fit in here at the higher levels, plus or minus 2 m (6½ ft): *C. c. racemosa*, *C. r. cordifolia*, *C. dahurica*, and *C. simplex* and its varieties, all with white flowers and maple-like leaves.

Before coming to the *pièce de résistance*, the hostas, let us look nearer to ground level. Here, there ought to be all the dicentras with finely cut contrasting grey-green leaves. *Dicentra formosa*, nearing 50 cm (20 in) high, in its best form 'Adrian Bloom', the white 'Alba' off-white 'Langtrees', redder 'Luxuriant' and 'Baccharal', and, shorter, the treasured 'Stuart Boothman', a misty pinkish crimson. *D. spectabilis*, the love-lies-bleeding, and its white form, belong here but I find them less strongly

perennial.

Corydalis solida, which pops up flowers like a fumitory and then disappears, fits here amongst *Vinca minor* 'Bowles Variety', a choice periwinkle. The most striking periwinkle is *V. major pubescens*, the dark star periwinkle.

Brunnera macrophylla, a strong perennial with broad rounded basal leaves, has blue forget-me-not flowers in an airy spread in spring and agrees with pink camellias. Height is usually about 45 cm (18 in). The tiarellas, or foam-flowers, make good neighbours to the brunneras, all with white flowers but later, in summer. *T. cordifolia* spreads, *T. wherryi* stays put, *T. polyphylla* stays put but seeds well and, *en masse*, attracts attention with its nice leaves, over which a cloud of minute, gnat-like flowers hovers.

The epimediums are very different with their pinnate leaves, some deciduous, some evergreen. Some hide their flowers and their old leaves should be clipped or strimmed in January to display the beauty of young leaves and flowers. They vary from 25 cm (10 in) to 45 cm (18 in) high. *E. grandiflorum* and its form 'White Beauty' are good and there are pink and purplish forms. *E. perralderanum* is a strong yellow. *E. pubigerum* is denigrated but I have a special liking for it because its handsome foliage is evergreen and its spikes of small creamy-white flowers rise well above it. *E. × rubrum* has pink-tinted young leaves and airy sprays of white-spurred crimson flowers.

Saxifraga fortunei is another ground-level companion with red-green leaves and sprays of white flowers very late in autumn. It almost heralds *Camellia* × *williamsii* 'November Pink' or *C. japonica* 'Gloire de Nantes'.

The family *Araceae* supplies some companions, arisaema, asarum, and arum.

Many hostas, funkias to our parents, like damp shady positions and so do slugs and snails. I have seen only two gardens in Cornwall with mature hosta leaves in pristine wholeness. One, Trebartha, has a bed of a large-leaved green species in a wood beside the cascading river Lynher and a sentinel flotilla of ducks on a nearby lake; the other, a formal garden near Restronguet Point, has sunken jars of beer.

Unless one is prepared to kill slugs and snails, forget hostas. There are pellets and tapes to distract the travelling slug or snail but one of the worst perforators is the little flat curled snail, which has no coat needing moisture by day and so stays up among the leaves. The watering can or sprayer with a liquid slug-killer must be used, if one can be sure of two dry days in a row! Fortunately a lot of camellias are grown on the acid Bagshot sand formation, which is totally lacking in lime. Snails are less trouble then but walls and mortar provide them with homes and calcium.

Few other herbaceous plants are receiving so much attention as the hosta. Books are written, catalogues swell and the price is often higher than that of the camellia. Photographs of beds of hostas, green, glaucous, gold, variegated, tall, dwarf, flowering, non-flowering, all together with the beds duplicated on either side of a pathway or drive, I find mentally and visually unacceptable – almost a breach of the peace!

That hostas are first-rate plants to associate with camellias I do not question. A glaucous, large-leaved hosta will harmonize with the evergreen foliage of a *japonica* camellia; equally the foliage of a variegated hosta will contrast successfully. They will also mix well with most of the herbaceous plants already mentioned, carefully graduating heights and widths, horizontals and verticals, rounds and spikes, and it is easy to conjure up groups of plants with great value to the garden.

Let the conjuring be done with simplicity and moderation. The hosta specialist carried away by the exuberance of the plants' morphology is liable to omit the grace and finesse of other foliage and flowers from the composition.

Earlier, the planting of *Cardiocrinum giganteum* in a camellia alcove was lauded. Here is a case where a simple association with one of the newer, large-leaved hostas could enhance the scene without destroying its simplicity. *H. sieboldiana* 'Bressingham Blue' at 1 m (3¼ ft) when in white flower, *H.* 'Krossa Regal', slightly shorter with lilac flowers, and *H.* 'Big Daddy', have glaucous leaves; *H.* 'Snowden' and *H.* Royal Standard' grow as tall, with white flowers, and green leaves. Keeping slugs from the hostas will do the cardiocrinums a good turn; they are also on the menu.

The boldness of *H.* 'Royal Standard' or *H. rectifolia* 'Tall Boy', both green leaved, contrasts well with the airy flight of the cimicifugas. *Geranium* 'Claridge Druce' looks well in front.

The little *Cardamine asarifolia* and *Saxifraga fortunei* would bear the company of a dwarf hosta. *H.* 'Ginko Craig', and *H.* 'Resonance' are dwarf with green and white leaves.

Permutations and combinations are endless. Suffice it to say that the most significant advance in hostas is, perhaps, the development of varieties with good heads of flower and fragrance above the bold leaves. My advice to the gardener bewildered by the number of varieties is to go and see them in one of the many gardens now specializing in them or in the National Collections at Wisley, Harewood House near Leeds, Kittock Mill, Carmunnock, Lanarkshire, Leeds City Council, or Apple Court, Lymington, Hampshire.

Finally, a word of warning. It is comparatively easy to devise planting schemes and put them into practice. Many of the tuberous or herbaceous plants will stay put for many years. Geraniums, for instance, such as *G. endressii*, will remain in place for twenty years but even they, in the end, will need dividing and re-planting elsewhere.

Re-planting is much more intricate and laboursome than planting and, if the example of geranium is followed, the replanter will be twenty years older than the planter! He or she cannot simply drop the plants into position charted on bare prepared ground as he or she did originally. One has to think out what is to go where, then lift the old plants, heel them in somewhere, dig the ground and prepare it with peat or other organic matter, fertilize it, cultivate it and then split and assemble the prepared plants in their new position and put them in.

All this in Britain, for example, in an unsettled climate! Much of it, too, while the adjacent camellias are in bloom!

THE SURPRISE ELEMENT

Whatever is planted in association with camellias, avoid placing the bushes in unbending lines so that what I have called the alcove effect is lost, for it engenders an element of surprise. If one rounds a bush or a group of camellias and finds a planting of erythroniums or *Cyclamen repandum* glowing just beyond, both the camellia and the lowlier plants generate greater interest and pleasure and, if the garden is not naturally divided into sections, this intimate method of grouping plants will captivate the visitor more than any spectacular mass of colour.

---

5. COMPANIONS FOR CAMELLIAS IN GREENHOUSES

Camellias in greenhouses are often seen in lonely splendour. What better! But if variety is preferred the choice of companion plants is a wide one ranging from the everyday cyclamen and primulas to some of the rarer plants cherished in Victorian times. Camellias in containers are usually summered outdoors and housed in late autumn or winter so that we are concerned with plants which will thrive in a temperature range between 3°C (37°F) and 26°C (80°F) with humid air and, possibly, shade, and flower between autumn and late spring. Cyclamen and primulas may need a little heat to keep the temperature up to 7°C (45°F) but the many spectacular modern selections of primroses and cinerarias will only need heat if in danger of damping off.

Among late spring-flowering shrubs correas are nearly hardy, beautiful and evergreen, with tubular or elongated bell shaped flowers: *C. alba* is white, *C. speciosa pulchella*, rose-red, and *C. × harrisi*, bright red (if one can find the true plant). The evergreen Australian epacris have similar flowers, some of them scented, and narrower evergreen leaves. *Daphne odora* will fill a greenhouse with fragrance and is hardy. The Victorians grew the evergreen shrubs agathosma, diosma and coleonema, including aromatic species which flower in winter or early spring. Potted plants of *Dicentra spectabilis*, the bleeding heart, and its white form 'Alba' also associate well with camellias.

The obvious plants to share their opulence with camellias are the cymbidiums, which enjoy the same regime and not the tropical heat which most people imagine they require. Their leaves and flowers provide a complete contrast from those of camellias and not all are unduly expensive.

One climber which deserves mention is *Lapageria rosea*, which loves the same conditions as camellias and has the same air of opulence about its red, pink, white, or striped bell-shaped flowers. One could be trained below the glass but it would limit the use of the house in summer.

CHAPTER THREE

CHOOSING THE BEST

Since the early days of Chandler in 1830, the camellia scene has been as changeable as the fashion for bedding plants. There is nothing static about it: the new varieties have multiplied and continue to do so.

The introduction of 'Drama Girl' in 1950, coming soon after the organization of the American Camellia Society in 1945 and the subsequent domination within the USA by the show bench, established a demand for large camellias. The use of gibberellic acid on flower buds to enlarge the size of flowers and improve their timing fostered the fashion.

The regular lists of show winners in the USA now includes a hard core of older camellias but each year more new introductions make their way into prominence. These have to be put on trial for some years before being sold in Britain, so the ultimate dimensions of the bush are often not known and in many cases the most that can be stated is an indication of vigour.

The most interesting hybrids are embracing such species as *rosaeflora*, *tsaii*, *pitardii*, *fraterna*, *taliensis* and *lutchuensis*, bringing in fragrance and dwarf habits. Dr Ackerman's first scented hybrid with *lutchuensis*, 'Fragrant Pink', is hardy in the south-west of Britain. Later hybrids 'Spring Mist', 'Scentuous', Domoto's charming hybrid, 'Scented Gem', and 'Baby Bear' and 'Snow Drop' from the Antipodes, are probably greenhouse camellias in Britain. There are other species recently introduced from China, such as *C. kissii* and *C. grijsii* which show great promise. Meanwhile, the yellow *C. chrysantha* stands aloof in the shadows!

Thirty species have been distributed outside China and are available in commerce. Over 200 species are known and have been classified in Asia.

CLASSIFICATION

The worldwide reference book for camellias is *Camellia Nomenclature* published biennially by the Southern California Camellia Society. It records and briefly describes the new registrations and lists the older varieties still in general cultivation. It is the Bible of the camelliophile and the reference source for flower show judges.

Camellias may be classified in two ways: by form of flower and by origin. First, let us consider classification in terms of the form of the camellia's flower. Here capital letters may be used to designate the form of the flower, as shown in the following list.

Class I – SINGLE
One row of not more than eight regular, irregular or loose petals around conspicuous stamens. Letter: S.

Class II – SEMI-DOUBLE
Two or more rows of petals with conspicuous stamens. Letters: SD.

Class III – ANEMONE FORM
One or more rows of large outer petals lying flat or undulating: the centre is a convex mass of intermingled petaloids or stamens. Letter: A.

Class IV – PEONY FORM subdivided into:
LOOSE PEONY FORM – loose petals which may be irregular with intermingled stamens and sometimes intermingled petals, petaloids and stamens in centre. Letters: LP.

FULL PEONY FORM – a convex mass of mixed irregular petals, petaloids, and stamens or irregular petaloids never showing stamens. Letter: P.

Class V – ROSE FORM DOUBLE
Imbricated petals showing stamens in a concave centre when fully opened. Letters: RFD.

Class VI – FORMAL DOUBLE
Fully imbricated with many rows of petals never showing stamens. Letters: FD.

The second way of classifying camellias, used in this chapter, is by origin. A classification enables us to separate the main types of camellia and to act as a guide in the choice of plants and their cultivation. *Camellia Nomenclature* classifies camellias by using the heading 'species' followed by the name of the key species such as *japonica*. This works with *japonica* and *sasanqua* and with *reticulata* so long as hybrids are omitted. *Camellia Nomenclature* sidesteps the issue by lumping *reticulata* hybrids in with the species, thus overlooking the fact that *C. saluenensis* is the dominant parent, and its hybrids with *reticulata* closely resemble × *williamsii* hybrids and perform like them in growth and may even excel them in hardiness. Hybrids between *C. reticulata* and *C. japonica* do closely resemble *reticulata* varieties.

I am, therefore, retaining the heading 'Japonica Camellias' for varieties of *C. japonica*, 'Sasanqua Camellias' for varieties of *C. sasanqua* and *C. hiemalis*, 'Reticulata Camellias' for *reticulata* seedlings and hybrids with *C. japonica*, and then using the heading '× Williamsii Hybrid Camellias and Allied Hybrids' for hardy camellias with *sasanqua*, *saluenensis* and *cuspidata* in their make-up. This puts together all those camellias with *C. saluenensis* and its progeny in their breeding, together with a few hybrids with *C. cuspidata*, such as 'Cornish Spring', which differ a little but have the same garden value as the × *williamsii* hybrids, as do the few hybrids between *C. reticulata* and *C. sasanqua* varieties.

For greenhouse cultivation some of the species and their new hybrids are becoming attractive, but they are not generally available in Europe and therefore largely excluded from this chapter.

The form of the flower given here is the form outdoors: where it is known to be different under glass this is mentioned and in warmer climates such as Australia, New Zealand and California that will be the outdoor form also.

CLASSIFICATION OF FLOWER SIZES	
Miniature	6.2 cm (2½ in) or less
Small	6.2–7.6 cm (2½–3 in)
Medium	7.6–10.1 cm (3–4 in)
Large	10.1–12.7 cm (4–5 in)
Very large	over 12.7 cm (5 in)

Time of flowering may be indicated by 'E' for Early, 'M' for Mid-season, and 'L' for Late. 'Early' covers flowering from late autumn to mid-winter; 'mid-season', late winter and early spring; and 'late' covers late spring to mid-summer. Camellias that flower in late autumn include the sasanquas, *oleifera* and the japonicas 'Gloire de Nantes' and 'Kramers Supreme', the × *williamsii* 'November Pink' and the hybrids 'Dream Girl' 'Flower Girl' and 'Show Girl'. At the other end of the season – May to July in England – several camellias will still be in flower at the end of May – 'Lady's Maid' 'Miss Universe', 'Joan Trehane', 'Mary Phoebe Taylor', 'Spring Festival' on into June, and 'Hawaii' carries flowers in shade on into July's hot days.

To summarize, the following selection of species/varieties is discussed under the following headings:

1. Camellia Species
2. Japonica Camellias
3. Sasanqua Camellias
4. Reticulata Camellias
5. × Williamsii Hybrid Camellias and Allied Hybrids

1. CAMELLIA SPECIES

C. chrysantha
The first to reach the west out of 11 camellia species with yellow flowers known to grow in China or Vietnam. It has large ribbed leaves with small single flowers, golden yellow with orange stamens, in the axils of the leaves, very often on the undersides of the stems. It is a small tree in the wild, growing in deep shade in semi-tropical conditions, and in Britain requires a greenhouse temperature well above freezing, with moist air. M.

C. crapnelliana (gigantocarpa)
In southern China and Hong Kong this is a tree up to 7 m (22 ft) high with large leaves and single white flowers up to 10 cm (4 in) across. Notable for its very large seed pods. E.

C. cuspidata
Widely distributed in China, introduced by E. H. Wilson, a thicket shrub as wide as 4.5 m (15 ft) and nearly as high, with narrow coppery-coloured young leaves up to 8 cm (3 in) long, and small single white flowers in their axils. Hardy in southern Britain and the parent of 'Cornish Snow', 'Cornish Spring', 'Spring Festival' and one or two other hybrids. A camellia with great promise for further breeding. M.

C. euphlebia
Similar in all respects to *C. chrysantha* but less vigorous. M.

C. forrestii
A twiggy bush with small leaves and flowers, whose principal merit is their large number and scent. M.–L.

C. fraterna
A considerable shrub with graceful stems, small leaves and fragrant single flowers, white with a slight shade of pink. Nearly hardy and best known for its hybrid, with the *japonica* 'Akebono', called 'Tiny Princess'. This has scented single white bells 4 cm across, with about 10 petals suffused with pink. M.

G. granthamiana
Found on the colder side of a mountain in Hong Kong, this magnificent camellia would probably succeed in good shelter in Cornwall, but elsewhere is a worthy greenhouse shrub up to 2 m (6 ft) or more in height and spread. The corrugated leaves are 20 × 4 cm (8 × 1½ in). The big, papery, flower buds look dry and dead in autumn but open into single white flowers 13 cm (5 in) across in mid-winter or early spring. Sobeck's variety has romneya-like petals, less pointed than the type. E.

Opposite: C. chrysantha *flowering in Nevill Haydon's nursery in New Zealand.*

Above: Camellia sinensis *(the tea plant) in flower.*

Lower: *Fine stamens are a feature of the semi-double 'Alexander Hunter'.*

'Berenice Boddy', soft looking but in fact very hardy and a graceful grower.

G. grijsii

Bushy to 3 m (10 ft) high, with leaves up to 9 cm (3½ in) long, and fragrant white single flowers 5 cm (2 in) in diameter. M.

G. japonica

From wild seed, a very variable single red with the well-known dark green broad leaves. At its best a fine flower some 10 cm (4 in) across. It makes a large bush 3 cm (10 ft) or more high and wide. E.

C. kissii

Known from Nepal to China, this makes a shrub or small tree up to 13 m (40 ft) high. It has small white fragrant flowers with notched petals in spring above small leaves up to 6 cm (2½ in) long. M.–L.

C. lutchuensis

So far the most used source of fragrance in hybridizing. A shrub or small tree from Formosa and the Japanese islands with small leaves and very fragrant small white single flowers. Dr Ackerman's hybrid with a *japonica*, 'Fragrant Pink', is hardy in Cornwall but requires sun to make it flower. M.

C. maliflora

A bush up to 2.4 m (8 ft) high or more on a warm wall, where it is usually found, this is now confirmed as a hybrid by Professor Chang Hung Ta. It has rose peony flowers 2.5 cm (1 in) across in mid-winter. M.–L.

C. oleifera

Long confused with *C. sasanqua* 'Narumi-gata', this slender-branched shrub or small tree flowers in late autumn or early winter with single white flowers up to 8 cm (3 in) wide. They are not long lasting and therefore of no value as cut flowers, but their scent is powerful and pleasing. Because of this species' extreme hardiness, hybrids have recently been raised from it in the USA. E.

C. reticulata

For a century confused with *C.r.* 'Capt. Rawes', this species is grown over a wide area in Yunnan for the oil from its seeds. George Forrest collected it between 1913–25 and there are trees 15 m (50 ft) high in Cornwall with single flowers 8 cm (3 in) across, variously coloured in shades of rosy-red. Some forms have been named. E.–M.

C. saluenensis

The key to hardiness and outdoor cultivation of camellias in Britain: grown from seed sent to J. C. Williams at Caerhays about 1917 from the same area of Yunnan as *C. reticulata*. It makes a big bush 3–4.5 m (10–15 ft) high and wide with dark leaves 6 cm (2½ in) long and half as wide. The flowers vary from white through all shades of pink to almost puce and are abundant in early spring. The seeds of the first × *williamsii* hybrids were taken from two bushes at Caerhays Castle in Cornwall. Les Jury in New Zealand used a different form. M.–L.

C. sasanqua

The favourite camellia of Japan with its hundreds of varieties. The species is a small tree with narrow leaves about 8 cm (3 in) long and small single white flowers, strongly scented, in late autumn. From seed the species varies greatly and it is the named varieties which are grown. E.

C. sinensis

The Chinese tea plant. In Cornwall outdoors a small stiff shrub with narrow leaves 10 cm in length, a rather pale green, and nodding small single white flowers in the axils of the leaves. E.–M.

C. taliensis

Introduced by Forrest in 1914 and planted in the great Cornish gardens where the single white flowers and round white buds stand out against the dark foliage in winter. The bushes grow 3–4 m (9–12 ft) high. E.

C. tsaii

This grows a little taller, with graceful branching and shining wavy leaves that are smaller than those of *C. taliensis*. The clusters of single white buds and flowers, 2.5 cm (1 in) across hang like racemes from the branches in winter sunshine in south-west Britain. It has the RHS Award of Merit as a cool greenhouse camellia. E.

C. yuhsienensis

Now reckoned to be a form of *C. grijsii*, with five widely separated white petals with notched ends. Fragrant, flowering in mid-spring. Considered to be to the great formal double japonicas of China what the field rose of Britain is to the hybrid tea rose of today. M.

2. JAPONICA CAMELLIAS

'Adolphe Audusson' France 1877
This vigorous red, raised in France in 1877, has long occupied first place in Britain. With irregular branching when young, it eventually makes a dense bush up to 5 m (16½ ft) wide by 4 m (13 ft) tall. The irregular semi-double flowers with few stamens are a good dark red, mid-season. Heavy crops of seedless fruits are borne. The bold leaves are dark shining green. M.

'Akashigata' ('Lady Clare') Japan 1887
Introduced from Japan a century ago, this large salmon-pink sometimes has a petaloid centre. The leaves are broad and large, the bush a great mound 1.5 m (5 ft) high when 3 m (10 ft) wide. M.–L.

'Alexander Hunter' Australia 1941
Notably upright moderate grower with bright crimson, single or semi-double flowers 10 cm (4 in) across, noticeable for their beautiful light stamens. M.

'Alice Wood' USA 1959
Not flowering when young but the compact bush, taller than wide, in the National Collection at Mt Edgcumbe has been solid with large rich dark red formal double flowers, which fall when over. L.

'Ann Sothern' USA 1960
A semi-double, 10 cm (4 in) across with pink, shading to white, petals, petaloides and stamens. Good foliage, bushy upright grower, flowers weather well. M.–L.

Above: 'Bob Hope', a most promising
modern dark red with dark foliage.

Opposite: 'Bob's Tinsie', a delightful
miniature anemone-form camellia.

'Annie Wylam' USA 1959
The fashion in camellias in the USA has swung away from mere bigness to the introduction of what we would call pastel and what they call 'sweet pea' shades. 'Annie Wylam' has been tested thoroughly and proved reliable and popular. It has a large deep rose-form double or peony flower with waved petals, clear pink shading deeper outwards. The leaves are 9 × 5 cm (3½ × 2 in), dark green on slender growth curving upwards. M.

'Apollo' – *see* **'Paul's Apollo'**

'Augusto L'Gouveia Pinto'
From Portugal in 1890 this *japonica* has large formal double smoky-red flowers which command high regard on the show bench. Moderate open grower. M.–L.

'Ave Maria' USA 1956
A miniature formal double light pink shading to a darker rose-bud centre. Bold, coarsely toothed dark leaves 9 × 6 cm (3½ × 2½ in). The majority of miniature camellias look better with small leaves to match the flowers, but in this case the effect of the bold foliage with the flowers peeping out is very attractive. An excellent tub plant. M.–L.

'Berenice Boddy' USA 1946
A graceful *japonica*, taller than wide, with dark glossy leaves and medium-sized, semi-double flowers in two shades of pale pink, darker on the outer petals. E.–M.

'Berenice Perfection' USA 1965
Not for outdoors but worth space in a greenhouse. An upright grower with soft pink, formal double flowers 10 cm (4 in) across, opening with a rosebud centre. M.

'Blaze of Glory' USA 1965
A *japonica* with handsome broad flat leaves, an open habit of growth, and large blood-red full peony flowers. E.–M.

'Bob Hope' USA 1972
A most promising medium-sized, dark black-red flat peony outdoors in Britain with glossy dark foliage and a compact habit of growth so far taller than wide. Under glass the flowers may not only be paler but also semi-double and large. M.–L.

'Bob's Tinsie' USA 1962
A seedling from 'Bokuhan'. A delightful miniature clear red anemone form camellia, with small leaves to match, on a close narrow upright twiggy bush. M.–L.

'Bokuhan' Japan 1930
An old Japanese miniature of great worth, regrettably also called 'Tinsie' in the USA, and parent of the above. This is a slow bushy grower, wider than tall, with small leaves and anemone form flowers with one row of red petals around an anemone centre of white petaloids. An excellent tub plant.

'C. M. Hovey' USA 1853
A ranging, large formal double showing

a stamen or two in a cool climate. Broad rounded petals, light salmon-tinted red. With its arching stems it may reach an impressive 4 m (13 ft) high by 3 m (10 ft) wide. M.

'Cardinal's Cap' USA 1961
A vivid red, close anemone form camellia with 9 cm (3½ in) flowers on every twig of a dense bush, higher than wide. M.–L.

'Charlotte de Rothschild' England *c.* 1930
Others may prefer 'Alba Simplex' or 'Devonia' but I have chosen this medium single white because I have observed its reliability over some 20 years. Six broad white petals open flat around a column of white stamens with pale gold anthers. The leaves are dark green, glossy, the bush is compact, and when 1.8 m (6 ft) high is as wide. M.

'Cheryl Lynn' USA 1965
Selected as a formal double because its medium sized sugar-pink formal double flowers shatter when over. A graceful grower, wider than tall. M.

'Commander Mulroy' USA 1961
Buds shaded pink open into white formal double flowers 8 cm (3 in) across. When 2.4 m (8 ft) high the dense upright bush is only 1.2 m (4 ft) across and this habit makes it excellent for growing as a luxurious hedge or a patio tub plant. The dark green glossy leaves are rounded 8 cm (3 in) long by nearly 6 cm (2¼ in) wide. Under glass the flowers have more pink. M.

'Contessa Lavinia Maggi – *see* 'Lavinia Maggi'

'Desire' USA 1977
This could be a world-beater! A fully formal double white with the outer ring of petals flushed with crimson. It makes a wonderful combination. Growth taller than wide. Broad glossy leaves. M.–L.

'Elegans' Chandler, London 1831
This large, rose-pink, anemone form camellia still holds its own on the show bench. It has notched petals and some white petaloids. The lax, wavy leaves are bold and distinctive on a spreading bush wider than tall. The leading shoot should not be pruned. This camellia is of special note for the high quality sports which have occurred in recent years. Of these 'Elegans Splendor', 'Elegans Supreme' and the white 'Shiro Chan' are fine under glass and the large frilly pink 'Hawaii' is the latest outdoor camellia still flowering in late summer in Britain. M.

'Elegans Supreme' USA 1969
A sport from Chandler's 'Elegans' with 10 cm (4 in) clear pink flowers, shading to a white frilled edging. The dark-veined petals encircle a small anemone centre. M.

'Gloire de Nantes' France 1895
Listed as a semi-double, but a rich rose-pink peony flower in Britain, often from late autumn onwards on a dense bush slowly growing to 4 m (13 ft) wide by 3 m (10 ft) high.

'Vittorio Emanuele II', a healthy veteran conserved at Porthpean House in Cornwall.

The formal double flowers of 'Rubescens Major' displayed above broad smooth leaves.

'Grand Prix' USA 1968
Worthily named, one of the best quality large semi-double red camellias for outdoors. A large, clear, light red flower over 11 cm (4½ in) across with broad petals around a bold set of stamens. The habit of growth is open, wider than tall, good free-standing or trained on a wall where the quality of flower will only be rivalled by the *reticulata* hybrid 'Royalty'. M.

'Grand Slam' USA 1962
In Britain outdoors this has a fine large dark red peony flower with a slight inclination towards semi-double or anemone form. The leaves are broad, dark green and pendent; the habit open and upright. Under glass the flower is massive with wavy petals and an anemone centre. M.–L.

'Guilio Nuccio' USA 1956
Named for a first rate Californian nurseryman. A glowing salmon-red, semi-double of great quality with waved petals around a good set of stamens. The leaves are long and deeply toothed and sometimes fishtail in form. Upright grower which tends to grow taller than wide. M.–L.

'Hagoromo' (Magnoliiflora') Japan 1886
This old camellia looks delicate but it is not. The flower is a graceful deep semi-double with narrow petals, white flushed pink. Its growth matches the flowers with open branching and narrow leaves. When 3 m (10 ft) high it is likely to be half as wide. M.

'Hana-Tachibana' Japan 1930
In Britain this old Japanese camellia is either formal or rose form double, deep pink, medium in size and very late to flower. The bush is slow growing, upright and, again, half as wide as high.

'Hawaii' USA 1961
A sport of 'C. M. Wilson' of the 'Elegans' family with 10 cm (4 in) peony flowers with white petals shading to pink, fimbriated and crimped. Last to flower, in July or August. M.–L.

'Henry Turnbull' Australia 1950
A simple, graceful, spreading grower. The eight broad petals of the single flower provide an elegant setting for a tall column of golden stamens. Its light pink counterpart, 'Jennifer Turnbull', is equally unsophisticated. M.–L.

'Janet Waterhouse' Australia 1952
Similar to 'Commander Mulroy' except that it is a pure white formal double in Britain. In a warmer climate it may be semi-double. M.

'Jingle Bells' USA 1958
Upright grower, taller than wide, with neat miniature, crimson, anemone flowers 7 cm (2½ in) across. 'Tinker Bell' is similar except for white or pale pink petals with crimson sectors or striped. E.

'Julia Drayton' USA 1840 as 'Mathotiana Rubra'
The name 'Mathotiana' spells confusion, for the empurpled, large, crimson formal double with bold foliage

has many names. It is best in a greenhouse or a warm sheltered position outdoors. A strong but not fast grower with bold foliage. M.

'Konron-Koku' Japan 1930
Again confusion reigns, for this red Japanese black-red can be found as 'Kouron-jura' or 'Nigra' or, possibly, 'Kuro-tsubaki'. It is possible that two camellias are being sold here, one with broad leaves, the other with narrower waved leaves but the flower in each case is black-red, a medium or small few-petalled formal double with occasional stamens. Growth is light and upright, twice as high as wide. M.

'Kramer's Supreme' USA 1957
The perfect model of a full peony camellia, rose-red, large, and in a greenhouse, spreading a carnation scent. In Cornwall it puts up a perfect flower or two for Christmas but properly it is mid-season. It is a compact upright grower, the height twice the width of a well-clothed bush.

'Lady Clare' – *see* **'Akashigata'**

'Lady Loch' Australia 1898
A sport form of the old 'Aspasia Macarthur' of 1850 which is still giving rise to such charming varieties as 'Margaret Davis' and 'Jean Clere'. It is a dignified candidate for association with *Cardiocrinum giganteum*, for its dark glossy leaves 9 cm (3½ in) × 6 cm (2⅜ in) curve downwards making a fine background. My bush is 3 m (10 ft) high by 1.8 m (6 ft) wide. The flowers are

nicely spaced out among the leaves, medium in size, peony form and picotee with dark-veined pink shading to a white fringe on broad reflexing outer petals around erect small central petals and petaloids. E.–L.

'Lavinia Maggi' (syn **'Contessa Lavinia Maggi'**) Italy 1860
Still one of the most popular striped formal doubles with a mixture of pink and carmine stripes on a white background. A bold upright grower to 3.6 m (12 ft) high and wide. This camellia is liable to sport red and any branch doing so should be cut out or it will take over the whole bush. E.–L.

'Lily Pons' USA 1955
Under glass, a single with long recurved petals: outdoors in Britain the most refined white semi-double in cultivation with tongue-shaped petals curving away from a good column of gold stamens. A light spreading bush with glossy wavy leaves 9 cm by 4 cm. M.–L.

'Little Bit' USA 1958
A small peony flower on a bush half as wide as high and with moderate vigour. The colour of the flower is debatable. Mine is red and white striped, with solid red sports occurring, but in New Zealand it is the other way round. Take your choice! E.–M.

'Lovelight' USA 1960
For such a large prolific, trumpet-shaped white this camellia weathers very well. Large in all its parts – flowers, leaves and upright bush. M.

Above: *'Ruddigore' will never win a show prize but has unbeatable flower-power.*

Opposite: *The massed striped flowers of Siebold's 'Tricolor' backed by its holly-like foliage.*

'Lucy Hester' USA 1959
This has the same great pendent glossy leaves as 'Drama Girl' and strong upright growth, but the form of the semi-double flowers is much superior, rich coral pink with darker veins, 12 cm (15 in) across. M.

'Magnoliiflora' – *see* **'Hagoromo'**

'Margaret Davis Picotee' USA 1982
One of the nicest sports from 'Aspasia Macarthur', a formal or rose form double white with a fine crimson edge on each petal. Not a precocious flowerer but worth waiting for. See 'Lady Loch'. M.

'Mary Costa' USA 1971
A moderate upright grower, well branched and prolific of unusual anemone-form flowers with white petals, around a variable centre of long creamy petaloides. M.

'Miss Universe' USA 1960
A good medium formal double white, with notched petals, weathering well partly because it flowers so late, well into summer. Spreading growth, perhaps twice as wide as high. L.

'Nuccio's Gem' USA 1970
Some succeed outdoors with this but here it is recommended for the greenhouse, as a formal double white, with a spiral arrangement of the petals. Moderate stiff open bush. M.

'Paul's Apollo' (**'Apollo'**) 1911
A reliable and generous red, semi-double with broad petals and a nice but relatively small cluster of gold stamens. Glossy dark green leaves. Good bushy grower. M.

'Primavera' USA 1950
A nice formal or rose form double white, 8 cm (3 in) across, which weathers better than most. A bushy grower, taller than wide. M.–L.

'R. L. Wheeler' USA 1940
A rumbustious camellia with very large rose-pink anemone form or peony flowers. The foliage is also large on an open spreading bush. Sometimes shows leaf mottle virus. M.

'Rubescens Major' France 1895
A formal double with large light red, slightly orange petals, flowering mid-season very freely on a dense, compact rounded bush with smooth, bold light green leaves. M.

'Ruddigore' USA 1980
A bright light red bushy semi-double to peony with fine cream stamens, which has one tremendous burst of flowers mid-season. Notable in the landscape, not a show flower. M.

'Shiro Chan' USA 1953
The most notable 'Elegans' sport for a greenhouse, with lovely white anemone flowers, up to 13 cm wide, with some pink touches. Compact growth. M.

'Taroan' (**'Yoibijin'**) Japan 1936
An old Japanese single, white or very pale pink notable for its low trailing

habit of growth and abundant crop of seeds. The leaves are dark and glossy: the plant will occupy 3 m (10 ft) or more if the occasional upright growth is cut out. Excellent for trailing over a large rock or a bank with azaleas. E.

'Tricolor' Japan 1832
Not only has this name been used for several camellias but this one, to which the name 'Siebold' is often attached, sports to pink, red and nearly white. It is distinguished from another old one with similar propensities by its holly-like crinkled leaves. It is a bushy grower, not over-vigorous but taller than wide. The flowers are single with red, pink and white stripes and of medium size. M.

'Vittorio Emanuele II' Italy 1867
A relatively few-petalled formal double with its basic white almost submerged in crimson stripes and splashes. Far more effective than 'Tricolor'. Free-flowering twiggy bush, a little taller than wide. Toothed rounded leaves 10 × 5 cm. M.

'Wilamina' USA 1951
A perfect miniature formal double, warm pink, edged paler, with round petals curving inwards. Rounded leaves and narrow upright growth. M.–L.

'Wm Bartlett' Australia 1958
Bushy rounded grower with simple, truly formal double flowers 8 cm (3 in) wide, white, powdered and lightly striped crimson. M.

'Yours Truly' USA 1949
A good sport of the century-old 'Lady

'Wilamina', so floriferous a miniature that it makes no cuttings without flower buds.

Vansittart' with flowers a little larger than 'Tricolor', mostly crimson-edged white, semi-double. Not a fast or very large grower. M.–L.

One highly specialized type of *japonica* camellia has not been mentioned. This is the Higo, a name derived from their original area in Kumamoto province in southern Japan where they are carefully preserved and used for bonsai. The flowers are single with a wide mass of 200 or more stamens which may occupy more than half the breadth of the flower. Unfortunately, leaf mottle virus is associated with age; these camellias are not generally available in Britain.

Above: *'Setsugekka' ('Fluted White'), a strong upright sasanqua with large white, semi-double flowers, with wavy petals.*

Opposite: *'Dr Clifford Parks'* (C. reticulata *'Crimson Robe'* × C. japonica *'Kramer's Supreme'*).

3. SASANQUA CAMELLIAS

The original name proposed by Thunberg for the camellia was Tsubaki, or Tsubakki, by which it is known in Japan, but Linnaeus did not approve and adopted the name *Camellia japonica*, which met Thunberg halfway but in Latin!

The Japanese have always preferred a more simple flower than the Chinese and it is the single forms of *C. japonica* which they grow. But they treasure still more their native, autumn-flowering *Camellia sasanqua*, first for the oil from its seeds and later on, but still some four or five centuries ago, for its evanescent, simple flowers which were more in accord with Zen Buddhism.

In recent times not only have the old sasanquas been brought together in Japan but they have become popular in Australia. In Europe, their flowering in time for frosts is a deterrent and the oldest specimens are in Italy. The later flowering types, differentiated as *C. hiemalis* or 'Kan Tsubaki', or the 'cold camellia', are here included with the earlier varieties.

Apart from the time of flowering, the sasanquas differ from the japonicas and *reticulata* camellias in other ways. They like full sun; they tolerate limy or alkaline soil, and they are more fragrant.

Their delicate flowers drop after a day or two, or shatter, but they are plentiful, given a sheltered position. Flowering during late autumn to mid-winter and requiring sun to enable them to do so, the flowers are so often pulped by even a light frost that they are of little value outdoors in Britain unless on a wall, in a warm, protected position, or in Cornwall or inner London. It is Australia which makes the greatest use of them as specimens, as hedge plants, as espaliers and as understock for grafting. But although the flowers are evanescent they are plentiful and they are fragrant so that the few sasanquas available in Britain can be used as pot plants or planted in greenhouses to cheer up the winter. Their use for bonsai points to an extended use as pot plants. The flowers are smaller than those of the *japonica* camellias.

Few of the 309 varieties in *Camellia Nomenclature* are available in Britain, so the list given is short and limited to those known to be available.

Sasanquas all have smaller flowers and the Large, Medium and Small imply a diameter half that cited in the initial classification of flower sizes.

'Bert Jones'
A large silvery pink semi-double with a long period of flowering. It makes strong long growths with impressive dark glossy leaves and is easily trained against a wall. L.

'Bonanza'
A moderate upright grower with large semi-double peony flowers, deep red in colour. E.

'Cleopatra'
Vigorous and bushy, with spreading, rather thin upright growth and small leaves. The flowers are early rose-pink

and semi-double. M.

'Dazzler'
Spreading with fan-shaped branches and bright rose-red semi-double flowers in late autumn. L.

'Hugh Evans' ('Hebe')
Strong grower, easily trained on a post or fence, with single pink flowers similar in shading to 'Cleopatra' but larger. M.

'Kanjiro'
In Australia, used as a stock for grafting. With resistance to a disease, *Botrytis cinnamomea*, this is vigorous and bushy with dark glossy foliage; its almost rose-form double flowers attract a lot of attention. M.

'Little Pearl'
Compact, upright grower with a picotee effect from its pink buds, opening into white semi-double flowers. L.

'Narumi Gata'
The most widely planted in Britain because it came in long ago as *oleifera*, which has flat white flowers, whereas this has cupped white flowers with pink edging. Upright growing and a good wall plant. M.

'Navajo'
Compact close growth with large wavy brilliant rose-red petals, zoned white around the stamens. M.

'Nodami Ushiro'
Handsome strong open growth with large leaves for a *sasanqua* and it buds

well. Single rose-pink flowers of good quality. M.

'Plantation Pink'
One for the milder places, a strong grower with large soft pink single flowers. M.

'Rainbow'
Lovely, almost purple buds and young stems, very free flowering with single white flowers, banded red. M.

'Shin Onome'
Large leaves, strong growth and large pale pink single flowers. Easily trained. M.

'Shishi Gashira'
Late (*hiemalis*) with broad glowing deep pink, semi-double, flowers. M.

'Snowflake'
Strong growing, spreading rather than upright, with large single white flowers. M.

'Tanya'
Very compact, slowly spreading, low grower with single deep rose-pink flowers. In Australia it is much used as a container plant. Good as bonsai. M.

'Yae Arare'
Large leaves, strong upright grower, making a handsome bush with large reflexed white petals, pink-tipped. M.

'Yuletide'
A good container plant with dense

bushy upright growth carrying late regular single flowers, with broad petals a glowing shade of pale red. L.

4. RETICULATA CAMELLIAS

Camellia Nomenclature for 1984 lists no less than 397 of these. Here are a mere sixteen:

'Arch of Triumph' USA 1970
A strong bushy upright grower with 17 cm (7 in) peony flowers with wavy petals which, seen outdoors, have an orange tint to the crimson rose. E.–L.

'Capt. Rawes' China 1820
The best known *reticulata* camellia in Britain, a carmine-rose pink full semi-double which is the glory of Joseph Paxton's greenhouse at Chatsworth. L.

'Dr Clifford Parks' USA 1971
Under glass a 15 cm (6 in) full peony flower dark rose-red. Leaves up to 14 cm (5½ in) long and 7 cm (2¾ in) wide. Open upright bush well branched and easy to train on a wall. M.

'Eden Roc' USA 1973
Outdoors a strong upright bushy grower with 14 cm (5½ in) semi-double rose pink flowers. Under glass the petals are craped. E.–L.

'Interval' USA 1970
Outdoors upright with large semi-

Opposite: 'Anticipation', showing its ideal growth habit for any garden.

double pink flowers with a good centre of cream stamens. Indoors darker clear pink and a flat flower with notched petals. M.

'K. O. Hester' USA 1972
A 17 cm (7 in) semi-double, described as 'orchid pink', of great substance and depth, with dark-veined petals as much as 7.5 cm (3 in) wide and attractively waved and notched. M.

'Lasca Beauty' USA 1973
The name derives from the initial letters of the Los Angeles State and County Arboretum where Dr. Clifford Parks bred this camellia. It is an open grower with large dark leaves 13 cm (5 in) by 8 cm (3 in) and clear deep pink trumpets 15 cm (6 in) wide by 8 cm (3 in) deep. M.

'Lila Naff' USA 1967
Outdoors a large-leaved open bush, broader than tall, with large bowl-shaped semi-double flowers, clear pink with a nice barrel of stamens. Indoors the petals are very large and recurve. M.–L.

'Lisa Gael' New Zealand 1967
Outdoors as upright as a Lombardy poplar with large, crimson-pink flowers like the common peony. Under glass it shows some stamens and white petaloides.

'Mandalay Queen' USA 1966
A more open grower than 'Arch of Triumph' with equally large peony flowers, deep pink. Indoors a very large semi-double with a small centre of

Above: *'Black Lace', a bushy 'Donation' ×
reticulata hybrid, is compact and neat.*

Opposite: *The × williamsii 'Bow bells'
usually rings in the New Year with flowers.*

stamens and darker, broad, veined and notched petals. M.

'Miss Tulare' USA 1975
A full deep light-red peony flower outdoors. Indoors fewer, larger, waved petals. M.

'Nuccio's Ruby' USA 1974
A large semi-double with the stamens enfolded by wide wavy dusky red petals. M.

'Otto Hopfer' USA 1970
Large light salmon, semi-double flowers with broad petals and a wide centre of pale yellow stamens. Outdoors a flat flower. Compact grower. M.

'Royalty' USA 1968
A tangled bush in the open with fine flowers, but on a wall a superb camellia with broad glossy leaves, easily trained and maintained. It covers itself with clear bright red, semi-double flowers, 15 cm (6 in) across. M.–L.

'Songzilin'
Better known as 'Pagoda' or 'Robert Fortune', who collected it in a Chinese port more than a thousand miles from its home in Yunnan. The best-known formal double crimson-red, *reticulata* camellia. M.–L.

'Wm. Hertrich' USA 1971
A tall, well-furnished bush always flowering well outdoors in Cornwall, even behind a north-facing wall. A cherry-red loose peony outdoors; a clear semi-double with a fine centre of butter-yellow stamens under glass. M.

The above is not an up-to-date list of *reticulata* camellias. There is little guidance in the new registrations: all are very large and very beautiful as these are! The demand in Europe does not warrant extensive trials.

5. × WILLIAMSII HYBRID CAMELLIAS AND ALLIED HYBRIDS

This heading includes the × *williamsii* hybrids, and their characteristics merit some exposition. They are easily recognized as camellias with their glossy, evergreen leaves but the leaves are generally smaller than those of *japonica* varieties.

The leaves of 'Lucy Hester' are the largest *japonica* leaves I can lay my hands on: 15 cm (6 in) long in the blade by 9 cm (3½ in) wide. 'Elsie Jury' has the largest leaves of the × *williamsii* hybrids to hand, 10 cm (4 in) long by 6 cm (2½ in) wide in the blade. 'Mary Larcom', a late Caerhays introduction, has the blade 9 cm (3½ in) long by nearly 6 cm (2½ in) wide, 'Ballet Queen' 8 cm (3 in) by 4 cm (1½ in), while 'Charles Colbert' goes down to 8 cm (3 in) by 3 cm.

The × *williamsii* hybrids are predominantly pink. There are a few whites but no certain first generation reds, two second generation, and one 'Donation' and *reticulata* cross, namely 'Jamie', 'Anne Hazlewood' and 'Black Lace' with 'Freedom Bell' of unknown parentage.

The × *williamsii* hybrids have a reputation for flowering very freely and for dropping their flowers when over. This is generally so with first generation × *williamsii* hybrids but not with second generation hybrids – nor with frosted flowers.

There is no doubt that the × *williamsii* hybrids have been the main stimulus of the camellia revival and are the front runners today in Britain.

'Anticipation' N.Z. 1962

First Class Certificate after trial at Wisley. A special camellia for small gardens or dot planting. When 3.6 m (12 ft) high, it may still be about 1 m (3¼ ft) wide and covered with very large crimson-rose peony flowers. I have measured flowers 15 cm (6 in) across in late spring. M.–L.

'Ballet Queen' N.Z. 1975

Under glass, that is in a warm climate, this has a rich salmon-pink peony flower. Outdoors it is a 10 cm (4 in) rose pink anemone-form flower with two rows of notched petals surrounding a central mass of petaloides of the same colour. An upright grower probably twice as tall as wide. M.

'Black Lace' USA 1968

Camellia × *williamsii* 'Donation' × *C. reticulata* 'Crimson Robe'. A hardy bright clear red formal double hybrid with typical small × *williamsii* leaves on a dense round slow-growing bush, its one fault being its failure to flower freely on a bush of normal selling size. It makes up for this later. Under glass it is semi-double. M.–L.

'Bow Bells' China 1925

'Bow Bells' is one of a little group of uncertain origin. It is an excellent camellia for any garden, precocious to the extent of flowering as a cutting. Flowers are warm pink, hose-in-hose, bell-shaped and open in the south as early as New Year's Day, continuing into late spring. The bush is compact, a little taller than wide and good, free-standing, for a north wall. E.–L.

'Bowen Bryant' Australia 1959

A well furnished bush, taller than wide with dark green leaves. One of the best of the × *williamsii* semi-doubles with boldly displayed, large bowl-shaped clear rose flowers. M.–L.

'Bridal Gown' USA

In California a formal double: in Britain a medium-sized white peony succeeding

Opposite: *'Cornish Snow', the best landscape white camellia from mid-winter to late spring.*

Above: *Illustrating the versatility of camellias, 'Spring Festival' grown as a standard by Mr John Lesnie in New Zealand.*

in the I.C.S. trials. Upright sturdy bush.
M.–L.

'Brigadoon' USA 1960
A very hardy deep pink large semi-
double which weathers well. Growth is
open, the bush as wide as tall. M.–L.

'Charles Colbert' Australia 1959
Not a show camellia because the
creamy-pink flowers have very few
stamens. The great merit of 'Charles
Colbert' is that it flowers freely and all
the flowers shatter when over. Semi-
double 10 cm (4 in). M.–L.
    This is a good example of how easy it
is to misjudge a camellia. Most
camellias grow upwards before
spreading and 'Charles Colbert' showed
every sign of being fastigiate but it has
not stayed narrowly upright and my
bush, about 20 years old, is now 4.5 m
(15 ft) high and 4 m (12 ft) wide.

'Cornish Snow' England 1951
A very hardy and prolific hybrid
between *Camellia saluenensis* and *C.
cuspidata*, the best landscape white
camellia throughout the winter and
early spring. The buds have a touch of
pink and open into 5 cm (2 in) white
single flowers. The new leaves are
copper-tinted, the bush rounded to
perhaps 4.5 m (15 ft) wide by 3.6 m
(12 ft) high. If it has a fault, 'Cornish
Snow' does not make a sturdy little bush
when young and its slender growths
should be tied to a cane when planted.
E.–L.

'Cornish Spring' England 1972

Camellia japonica 'Rosea Simplex' × *C.
cuspidata*, raised at Tregrehan in
Cornwall. Upright and very bushy with
4.5 cm (1¾ in) deep pink bell-shaped
flowers in great profusion. The leaves 6
× 4 cm (2½ × 1½ in) are mid-green with
a matt surface. Associates well with
Pieris 'Wada's Pink'. M.–L.

'Daintiness' N.Z. 1962.
Not a mass of flowers like 'Donation'
but an open bush, 2.1 m (7 ft) wide when
3 m (10 ft) tall, with durable 10 cm (4 in)
rose-pink, semi-double flowers with
cream stamens, gracefully spaced on
horizontal branches. M.

'Debbie' N.Z. 1965 Award of Merit 1971
A robust round bush, with typical ×
williamsii leaves, probably growing
4.5 m (15 ft) high and wide, liable to
open its first deep full peony flowers
10 cm (4 in) wide, in mid-winter and
continuing into early summer. They are
rose-pink and fall whole when over,
carpeting the ground with colour.
    'Debbie' was raised by Les Jury from
C. saluenensis × *C. j.* 'Debutante'. His
brother Felix made the same cross with
a different form of the species and his
clone is named 'Debbie Felix'. It is very
close to Les's 'Debbie' but slightly
better, with a fuller flower, and it is
earlier to come into full bloom as a more
compact and upright bush. E.–L.

'Donation' England 1941
The most popular camellia in Britain.
Rarely more than 2.4 m (8 ft) wide when
4.5 m (15 ft) high. In the open it is
covered with large semi-double pink

'Tiny Princess', a hybrid of C. fraterna, *light and airy in a hanging basket in New Zealand.*

flowers. In light shade the colour is deeper, the quality of flowers better and they last longer. M.–L.

'Dream Boat' N.Z. 1976
Free-flowering pink formal double with flowers 9.5 cm (3¾ in) across which shatter when over. The leaves are 9 × 4.5 cm (3½ × 1¾ in), curved inwards. A bushy grower wider than tall. M. In New Zealand 'Dream Boat's' petals have a rolled edge. In Britain they do

not and the flower is perfectly natural – and naturally perfect.

'Dream Girl' USA 1965
This is a hybrid between *Camellia sasanqua* 'Narumi-gata' and *C. reticulata* 'Buddha' and it is one of three crosses achieved by Mr. Howard Asper with some difficulty. The others are 'Flower Girl' and 'Show Girl' and all are shades of pink, and flower from early winter to early spring. Under glass the

Above: *'Elegant Beauty', a worthy* ×
williamsii *descendant from Chandler's
'Elegans', good on a north wall.*

Opposite: *'Elsie Jury', a bit temperamental
but at its best in Lancashire or London; a
slender bearer of the finest peony flowers.*

flowers are heavily scented: outdoors the scent is only noticed on a mild damp day. The flowers are semi-double 13 cm (5 in) across and shatter when over. They weather well and the parentage indicates that these are good camellias for south walls. Growth is open.

'E. G. Waterhouse' Australia 1954
Not quite so fastigiate as first appeared but still a compact upright pyramid suitable for a sunny position outdoors or as a pot plant for the porch or patio. The flowers, of medium size, are formal double, a warm shade of pink, and shatter when over. M.

'E. T. R. Carlyon' England 1972
In Britain a good white peony with medium sized flowers wreathing long arching branches. L.

'Elegant Beauty' N.Z. 1962
A × *williamsii* hybrid with *Camellia japonica* 'Elegans' and one of the most floriferous camellias. The colour is the deep pink of 'Elegans'. The narrower × *williamsii* leaves are coppery when young on arching growths. It may be necessary to prune these back on a young plant to get a balanced bush. Excellent trained on a shaded wall where the flowers last longer. To train it shorten growths back to side shoots as soon as flowers are over. M.–L.

'Elsie Jury' N.Z. 1964
Awarded the First Class Certificate in 1975 after trial at Wisley. The 13 cm (5 in) blooms are clear pale pink, anemone or peony form. The outer ring of overlapping petals, deeply cleft, surrounds a centre of waved petaloids and stamens. Growth is normally open and upright, good for small gardens. Not always hardy in the north of England. In that situation give plenty of sun and phosphate to ripen the buds well. M.–L.

'Francie L.' USA 1964
Its parentage is *Camellia saluenensis* 'Apple Blossom' × *C. reticulata* 'Buddha', which combine three species in its make-up. It has long narrow leaves like a peach, but with the texture of a *reticulata* camellia, and it makes long fan-shaped branches, ideal for training on a wall. At Southampton it flourishes on a south-east wall, at West Hill in Devon on a west wall and at Trehane in Cornwall on a north wall. It is capable of covering a space in excess of 4.5 m × 6 m (15 ft high by 20 ft wide) and flowers abundantly over a long period with very large 14 cm (5½ in) semi-double crimson-rose flowers. This camellia could transform many a dull wall in central London. M.

'Free Style' USA 1980
This camellia was named so by its raiser, David Feathers, because of the freedom with which it flowers and the informality of the blooms, which are semi-double, 13 cm (5 in) wide with 15 notched petals, some rabbits' ears and yellow stamens. These frilled petals are pale pink with a picotee edge. This camellia has a *reticulata* pollen parent and came to notice because of its extreme hardiness. After a very severe winter it stood a

pillar of colour when all around it had lost their flower buds. It grows narrowly upright but, after the defection of 'Charles Colbert', I am not using the word fastigiate! M.

'Freedom Bell' USA 1963
A chance seedling which looks like a × *williamsii* hybrid and is very hardy. A fine brilliant camellia for smaller gardens, slowly making a close rounded bush, here after 20 years 2.1 m (7 ft) wide and tall. Its brilliant red semi-double flowers 9 cm (3½ in) across, with twelve narrow incurving petals, cover the bush from early spring to early summer and clash with pink. A neutral alliance with a *Mahonia media* or a pieris is good. The glossy green leaves are in scale with the flowers and bush. E.–L.

'Galaxie' USA 1963
The only significant striped × *williamsii* hybrid, at its best when the flowers are partly open, showing a rose-bud centre, before turning into a formal double, pale pink with darker veins and notched petals striped with light red. A small-leaved bush very near to 'Freedom Bell' in size. M.–L.

'Garden Glory' USA 1974
Few other formal, double camellias flower from mid-winter to the end of spring. The flowers are rich clear pink, medium sized, formal double with broad petals, cupped inwards and slightly notched. Bushy slow grower, ten years after planting 1.8 m (6 ft) high and wide. The foliage is not brilliant and it is advisable to feed this camellia in spring.

'Gay Time' N.Z. 1970
A quiet camellia for a shady nook with variable flowers, mostly loose peony or semi-double, with orchid-pink, lavender-tinted waved petals. An open bush which grows as wide as it does tall. M.–L.

'George Blandford' Caerhays 1958
C. saluenensis × *C. japonica* 'Akashigata' ('Lady Clare'). A true flat peony flower up to 13 cm (5 in) across, bright crimson pink without the blue of its fellow seedling, 'Caerhays Castle'. It makes a big round bush up to 3.5 m (12 ft) high and wide. E.–L.

'Innovation' USA 1965
Not a show flower but one of the very hardy hybrids with a *reticulata* pollen parent. It grows into a big round bush, probably 3.5 m (12 ft) high and wide, and flowers early with weather resistant full peony flowers 11 cm (4½ in) wide and 5 cm (2 in) deep, deep rose crimson with darker veining and a few gold stamens. E.–L.

'Inspiration' England 1954
This has come out top for reliability in the International Camellia Society trials in the Midlands and north, Edinburgh and Belfast. In growth dimensions it parallels 'Donation' to which, in the quality and spacing of its bright deep pink 10 cm (4 in) semi-double flowers, it is much superior. It flowers a few weeks earlier. E.–L.

Above: 'Francie L', *one of the best camellias for training on an extensive wall.*

Opposite: 'Freedom Bell', *the first red ×* williamsii *hybrid, excellent for a small garden.*

'J.C. Williams' Cornwall 1940
Every year this lovely camellia, fitly
named for the raiser of the first of the ×
williamsii hybrids, is so crowded with
multiple flower buds that it is rare to
find cuttings without them. The flowers
are single, pale pink, with broad,
attractively waved petals. The bush in
sun is dense but puts forth long,
graceful, fan-shaped branches which
makes this camellia a good option for
training on a north wall. E.–L.

'Joan Trehane' N.Z. 1980
A fine late camellia which was named
only because Les Jury, who raised it,
and his wife, saw it in my garden. Spring
in New Zealand comes too quickly for
it. Here it is in flower from mid-spring
to early summer, at its best with some
shade when the rose form double
flowers reach 12 cm (4¾ in) across,
coloured rose with 35 petals, a few
rabbits' ears and cream stamens,
making a fairly flat flower, weathering
well. Dark green leaves 9 cm (3½ in) by
5 cm (2 in). Prolific grower, for several
years twice as tall as wide.

'Jubilation' N.Z. 1978
A rose form double, of medium size
with notched bright pink petals
outdoors, paler with central rabbits'
ears under glass. The bush is rounded,
1.8 m (6 ft) wide when 1.5 m (5 ft) high,
with the tips of the lateral growths
turning downwards. It has a
concentrated burst of flowering mid-
season. For comparison 'Jury's Charity'
alongside my bush is, at the same age,
3 m (10 ft) wide by 2.1 m (7 ft) high, a

very prolific late camellia.

'Julia Hamiter' USA 1964
An eye-catching seedling from
'Donation', an open spreading bush
more like a *japonica* in growth and
foliage. The flowers are flat except for
the petaloids and rabbits' ears in the
centre. They are surrounded by two
rows of pale apple blossom pink, frilled
petals making up a loose peony flower
10 cm (4 in) across. Unless this camellia
has the ripening effect of plenty of sun it
will not complete its flower buds. M.

'Jury's Yellow' N.Z. 1976
The flowers are almost identical with
those of two japonicas, 'Gwenneth
Morey' and 'Brushfield's Yellow', none
of them truly yellow like the species
Camellia chrysantha. Each has a wide
anemone centre of yellow petaloids
which reflect their colour on to the outer
ring of white petals. I rate this the best
of the three because it is more prolific
when young and, having 25% of *C.
saluenensis* in its make-up, it weathers a
little better. Under glass it is a full
peony flower. E.–L.

'Lady's Maid' Australia 1960
A clean bush; my twenty-year old plant
is 4.5 m (15 ft) wide and tall. It makes a
tremendous show with its 10 cm (4 in)
clear pink, bowl-shaped flowers which
are pendent and shatter when over.
One of the best late camellias. Semi-
double, L.

'Leonard Messel' England 1958
A hybrid between the wild form of

Camellia reticulata and *C.* × *williamsii* 'Mary Christian', hardy up into Scotland. This is a prime example of the effect of climate on the form of flowers. Under glass it is a slightly larger rose semi-double with a regular and conspicuous centre of stamens. Outdoors the flower is a loose peony with no stamens showing. In Cornwall I have a bush some twenty years old, rounded, 3 m (10 ft) or more wide and 4 m (13 ft) high with matt green leaves up to 9 cm (3½ in) long by 4 cm (1½ in) wide. The flowers are large, mid-season, rose with a hint of apricot. In theory this should be a tender camellia but the subtle influence of *C. saluenensis* through its pollen parent 'Mary Christian', makes this one of the hardiest and most successful in Britain at least as far north as Perth. M.

'Mary Larcom' England 1961
One of the later × *williamsii* hybrids from Caerhays, a good single pink 9.5 cm (3¾ in) across with broad leaves (see p. 00) on a stout round bush 4 m (13 ft) high by 3.6 m (12 ft) wide at about 20 years of age. M.–L.

'Mary Phoebe Taylor' N.Z. 1975
This is one of the largest of the × *williamsii* hybrids with very large peony flowers of a warm shade of pink. If the flowers are heavyweight they are displayed lightly by the branching which is graceful and out-reaching, making a wide-spreading bush with slender leaves 9.5 cm (3¾ in) long and only 3.5 cm (1⅜ in) wide, the tips curving sideways and down. M.–L.

'November Pink' England 1951
This would not get in for its show quality: it is about on a par with a briar-rose in quality and its arching slender growths, but it cheers up the late autumn and winter with cascades of single rose-pink flowers of medium size. For propagation one has to be quick, for it breaks into secondary growth very fast and regularly as summer declines. E.–M.

'Satan's Robe' USA 1965
A brilliant hybrid between *Camellia* 'Satan's Satin' and *C. reticulata*. The 25% of *C. saluenensis* in 'Satan's Satin' gives it a fair degree of hardiness. It is one of the most brilliant red semi-double camellias in existence, with flowers of good size in great profusion on downward curving branches. The foliage is *japonica* like, and the bush strong growing, slightly wider than high. M.

'Senorita' N.Z. 1975
One of Les Jury's later seedlings, a neat upright grower with very deep peony flowers 10 cm (4 in) across, semi-double under glass. A specially lively deep pink with golden stamens showing between the petals. Leaves glossy 8 cm (3 in) by 4 cm (1½ in). M.–L.

'Spring Festival' USA 1975
An exceptional hybrid between *Camellia cuspidata*, with its small white flowers, and a formal double *japonica*. It has made its mark as a fastigiate evergreen with late spring to early summer formal double pink flowers 6 cm (2½ in) across, marvellous in a tub

Above: *Few camellias give so long-lasting a display as this × williamsii 'Garden Glory'.*

Opposite: *'Inspiration' more than equals 'Donation' in the quality of its flowers and is earlier.*

Opposite: *The very hardy 'Leonard Messel' is here shown as it is under glass. Outdoors it is a peony camellia.*

Above: *The graceful spreading growths of 'Mary Phoebe Taylor' prevent its large flowers looking unwieldy.*

or urn. The young foliage is copper-coloured. It must have plenty of sun and it is very, very lovely. The form of branching of 'Spring Festival' is different from that of *C.* × *williamsii* 'Anticipation', and a possible weakness, for the lateral branches are ascendant and may be pushed down by snow and if unable to regain position they must be cut back. I have not tried it but it may be good practice to spur back the side shoots regularly to strengthen the structure of the bush and retain its fastigiate habit. With me, at 3.6 m (12 ft) high it is 1.8 m (6 ft) wide with very dense growth. L.

'St. Ewe' England 1947
A favourite among the Caerhays × *williamsii*, with glossy foliage and bright rose-pink single trumpets, wider, larger and darker than those of 'Bow Bells' and only days behind it in time of flowering. E.–L.

'Tiptoe' Australia 1965
A natural hedger. At 20 years old, mine (as yet unclipped) is 2.4 m (8 ft) high, and 1.5 m (5 ft) wide at the bottom, with a natural taper to the top. The leaves are glossy green, 9 cm (3½ in) long by 4 cm (1½ in) wide and the flowers are medium-sized pale pink semi-doubles; they have one fault, they do not drop off and have to be shaken or picked off. Mine are planted 75 cm apart. E.–L.

Opposite: *'Satan's Robe'. Few camellias make a more brilliant display than this hybrid, which combines the species japonica, saluenensis and reticulata.*

'Water Lily' N.Z. 1967
A lovely formal double, true to its name in the appearance of its 13 cm (5 in) flowers with their fresh pink, almost translucent petals. Growth is slender, making a cascade of flowers in mid-season. These flowers drop when over. M.

'Wilber Foss' N.Z. 1971
A rich claret-coloured, full deep peony 13 cm (5 in) across and half as deep, with broad thick petals and stamens between. A dense glossy green bush. At 20 years 2.4 m (8 ft) high and wide. M.–L.

The above are but a few camellias to whet the appetite. There are thousands more and nearly 200 new ones are registered each year. Information about these comes in the last chapter.

As an addendum, a word about the use of camellias indoors. Bought as a house-plant a camellia will be a great disappointment in a centrally-heated dry room, so unlike its forest home. The flowers wilt in a very short time in a hot, dry atmosphere. Those most likely to succeed are the *sasanqua* camellias, the flowers of which are fragrant and short-lived anyway, but the pot should be stood on wet pebbles or coarse sand to put some moisture into the air around the plant.

In a cold, glassed-in porch or sun-room they will make a brave show, particularly the *reticulata*. The same applies to cut branches. The life of single flowers is prolonged by floating them in a shallow dish of water.

CHAPTER FOUR

GENERAL CULTIVATION

Attending flower shows in Cornwall and London, and exhibiting camellias, I learn most of the problems encountered by people growing camellias in gardens and greenhouses.

The problems are few. The most common in planting outdoors is to choose a sheltered position near a wall or hedge and then to fail to remember that the bush will not be able to get a normal ration of rain to enable it to make and hold on to its flower buds. The second is failure to give the bush enough room and the question then is 'Can I cut my camellia?'. For the people who ask 'What should I feed my camellias with?' I usually suggest Vitax Rhododendron and Azalea fertilizer.

For those growing camellias in pots or some other container, by far the most common trouble arises from failure to protect the roots from frost. They must not get frozen solid. In late winter/early spring the owner is gleeful because the unprotected camellias have come through with all their leaves and flower buds. In mid-spring, when the sun has gained power, all is gloom because the plants are brown and dead. Another sudden death problem might happen when feeding pot-grown camellias after the end of late summer (August in Britain). The reason for this is that during active growth the plant is using the chemicals dissolved in the water but, as soon as winter approaches, it stores what is needed for the leaves and flower buds and any surplus builds up in the compost to a harmful and, finally, lethal level. There is no resurrection!

This vital subject of cultivation is here divided into six sections, dealing first with the indicators which enable one to decide whether to grow camellias in the ground outdoors or not; next the preparation of the soil and planting; then pruning and training; followed by methods of cultivation, cultivation under glass or plastic; and pests, diseases and disorders.

THE SITE AND CLIMATE

Bear in mind that camellias are evergreen trees and shrubs of mountains and forests in China and Japan. They need a well-drained, organic and acid soil.

The simplest way to check whether the soil is acid is to look around at what grows wild and what grows in other people's gardens.

If the site is in an area of heathland dominated by heather, gorse and broom, it will have acid soil. Gardens nearby should have rhododendrons and azaleas. *Rhododendron ponticum* is likely to be wild near or in settlements. If the site has been used for agriculture it will almost certainly have been limed and it is essential to verify this. There are two classic weed indicators for acid soil. If the bright yellow flowered corn marigold is there the soil is likely to be acid. Likewise if the more humble corn spurry grows *en masse* with its whorls of thread-like leaves and tiny white flowers just above ground level. The soil can be too acid for camellias and one indicator plant to tell you this is the common bilberry or whortleberry.

Retailers of sundries for gardens usually sell quite simple and cheap kits for checking whether the soil is suitable. The symbol pH denotes acidity or alkalinity of the soil. A neutral soil is pH 7.0. Below pH 7.0 the soil is acid and above it alkaline. For camellias it should be acid within the range pH 5.5–6.5. The test kit will generally show the pH by the colour of a fluid in a glass tube into which the soil sample has been dropped. If the soil is basically unsuitable because it is on limestone or chalk, or calcareous clay, it is practically impossible to grow camellias in it. Alternative methods to circumvent this will be dealt with later. If the soil is basically acid but the pH has been raised above 6.5 by liming, the pH can be lowered by using aluminium sulphate, as for blueing hydrangeas, or crude sulphur, or, more safely, crude ferrous sulphate. Pure ferrous sulphate from the chemist is expensive; the crude chemical should be available from garden centres. To reduce the pH from 8.0 to 6.0 requires 8 kg (18 lb) per 9.2 m² (100 sq ft), from 7.5 to 6.0 requires 7.4 kg (16 lb) and from 7.0 to 6.0 requires 4.2 kg (9.4 lb).

Sprinkle the chemical over the soil, water it in and test the pH a few days later. If there is a risk of calcium being washed or blown (agricultural use) into the area, spread a little ferrous sulphate each year. The pH should not rise because ordinary rain is normally acid at pH 5.75.

If the pH is too low, as in areas of Dartmoor, Exmoor and Bodmin Moor, the bilberry may indicate it in the wild nearby and a camellia will show it by making long smooth growths with few lateral branches or flowers. Camellias, like bilberries, are calcifuges, that is they do not tolerate the calcium which is dominant in lime or chalk and it, therefore, must not be used to raise the pH. The correct chemical, sold by most garden centres, is magnesian limestone.

There are tables available for the quantity of lime to be used but not for the magnesian limestone. As a guide the following is quoted: 'to raise the pH from 4 to 5.2 spread 300 g (11 oz) per m² (sq yd) of magnesian limestone.'
Now, having taken a preliminary look at the soil, let us consider the climate.

Camellias will grow and flower outdoors in the British Isles between the south coast and central Scotland and Northern Ireland, subject to the varietal limitations already referred to in 'Choosing the Best'. The limiting climatic factor is the adequate ripening of the year's growth and flower buds to withstand the winter cold. Britain is at a disadvantage here because it does not have the reliable hot summer which makes camellias so much hardier in China and the USA, Australia, New Zealand and the Mediterranean littoral.

Cornwall and Southern Ireland come nearest to the ideal climate, with damp sea breezes and, most years, enough sun to set the flower buds and open them in spring; and traditionally, a mild winter. The greatest expert on camellias in Britain, Mr. Charles Puddle, said to me that 'camellias can succeed on one site and fail half a mile (0.8 km) away'. To illustrate this, Caerhays Castle has the premier garden in Cornwall growing all sorts of tender trees and shrubs on the south coast where a small river flows into Porthluney Cove. Half a mile westward is a coastal frost pocket so deadly that a pieris cannot be grown at all. Cold air is heavier than warm and flows down into valleys which may have a frost as frequently as nine months of the year – no climate for a camellia or a rhododendron. So seek out warmer micro-climates.

In a very hard winter, such as 1962–63, when the sun shone fiercely on evergreens frozen to the tips of the roots, preventing sap rising, camellias, privet and laurels died as much from desiccation as from the cold. Thatching them over with straw might have saved them.

Camellias may lose flower buds or,

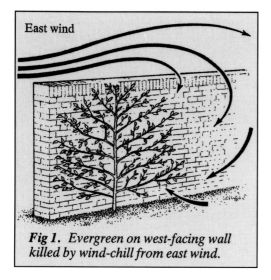

Fig 1. *Evergreen on west-facing wall killed by wind-chill from east wind.*

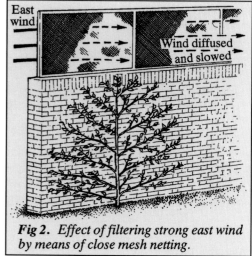

Fig 2. *Effect of filtering strong east wind by means of close mesh netting.*

later, produce damaged flowers with black stamens after the temperature has fallen below −11°C (12°F) for a few days. Young plants may be killed at −16°C (3°F) and established plants cut to ground level. Even if these look dead they should be left alone at least until late summer or autumn by which time new shoots may have grown from ground level. If the plant is grafted check that the shoots are not from a *japonica* stock and then cut away the old dead top. Camellias may, bravely, form flower buds in a poor summer. If this is followed by a warmer autumn these flower buds may revert into growth. In the case of *japonica* camellias this may mean no flowers next spring: the × *williamsii* hybrids usually manage to perfect both the secondary growths and the flowers.

Remember that roots, not only of camellias, but double primroses too, and other plants, are killed at much

higher temperatures than the shoots so plants in containers should be plunged in the ground or otherwise insulated from frost.

Camellias do not mind wind but they hate draughts. Plants in a channel between house and fence or near the front or back porch, or under a London office block or, for example, at the Department of the Environment, where the wind whistles round the corner, may show their discomfort with brown leaves, or leaf edges. Move them.

An east wind-frost is an exceptional killer. The velocity of the wind increases the penetration and intensity of only a few degrees of frost. Bark-split is one of the consequences. A wall alone may be a disadvantage (Fig. 1). A screen of plastic wind-break or very fine mesh wire-netting on top of the wall helps by filtering the wind and slowing it down (Fig. 2).

The alternative to the damp air of the

sea or lakeside is shade, preferably high shade from tall trees. The further north in Britain the more sun and shelter are needed. Most camellias can be grown in the shelter of walls – east if there is a screen to intercept cold winds, south if there is light shade for at least the hottest hours of the day, west-facing the best, and north-facing for some of the × *williamsii* hybrids. Remember that normal rainfall may not reach plants against walls in summer. This is the principal cause of flower buds dropping in November. A good soaking once a week is the answer.

SOIL AND PLANTING

There are large areas of acid soils in Britain. The igneous rocks of Cornwall, Devon, Cumbria, Wales, and Scotland have mostly acid soils above them and, except where the wind has blown inland sea sand with shell, camellias grow well. The heavy Culm measures in north Cornwall and west Devon are difficult to drain.

The Bagshot sand of Surrey and parts of Hampshire and Dorset is just the opposite. The acidity is there but very little else other than a thin layer of heather peat on top and, perhaps, again, below an iron pan or callus a spit (spade's depth) or more down. This needs breaking up but without bringing it to the surface. Long ago in Dorset I did this by the light of a Tilley lantern! Nowadays there would be a machine.

To bring them near to the condition of a forest floor most soils need improvement. This is where cow manure comes in. I know it is used as a mulch in Australia in a hotter climate where bacterial activity is faster. In Britain its use, in my opinion, should be to improve the soil a season ahead of planting, not as a direct mulch for the plant. Bagshot sand heathland is totally fungoid. There is no bacterial activity. One reads prescriptions for the use of well-rotted cow manure. Where is it? Our forebears knew it as a peat-like substance for general use. Today the best obtainable may have been stacked for a season at the most. It will be cold and sticky. That is why I recommend digging in a heavy dressing during the winter or spring before planting the following autumn or spring. During the summer it will rot down within the soil, promoting bacteral activity, fertility and texture.

Camellias do require a minute quantity of calcium and the straw in the manure will supply some.

In London and other cities cow-keeping was given up fifty years ago and some alternative to cow manure must be used. Sphagnum peat is the most practicable alternative.

Plants are sold in containers – pots, plastic bags, tubs – and can be planted in the autumn if grown in the open in the nursery. Most are not and, increasingly, they are planted in spring, after the danger of severe frost is over. If bought early to get all the flowers, and planting is then delayed, keep the plant in the coolest place available.

Planting can be a problem. I once had to diagnose the cause of death and found the rootball 20 cm (9 in) down. Its top must always be level with the surface of the soil. So here is a routine method of planting.

Mark out a square metre or yard. Clean off any weeds and spread medium grade sphagnum peat 8 cm (3 in) deep over it. Dig out the top spit, peat and soil, putting it in a heap alongside, so mixing them partly. Break up the sub-soil with a fork, leaving it in place, and then replace the top spit, thereby completing the mixing of peat and topsoil,

level, and tread fairly firm. At planting time spread 120 g (½ lb) of John Innes base fertilizer over the area, fork it in, tread lightly and then take out a hole for the plant. If the roots are young and all fibrous the plant may be tapped out of its pot and dropped into a hole to fit it so that the pot soil surface is level with the firmed soil after treading lightly (Fig. 3).

If the plant is pot-bound and has a dominant thick root circling the root-

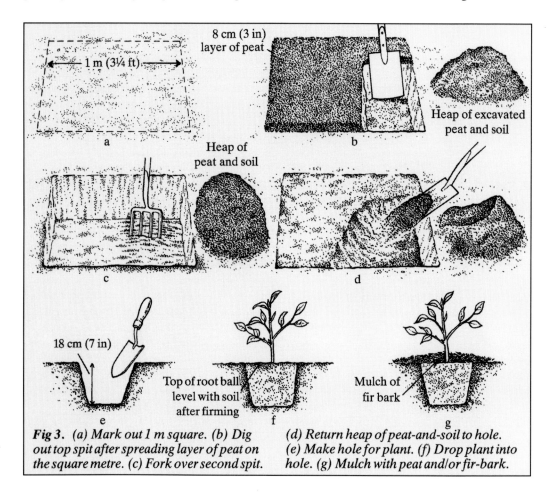

Fig 3. *(a) Mark out 1 m square. (b) Dig out top spit after spreading layer of peat on the square metre. (c) Fork over second spit. (d) Return heap of peat-and-soil to hole. (e) Make hole for plant. (f) Drop plant into hole. (g) Mulch with peat and/or fir-bark.*

ball, enlarge the hole so that the thick root can be teased out and spread out in it. If the roots are too tightly bound to allow this, just take a knife and cut down the side of the rootball regardless. Failure to do this may result in root strangulation, the damage from which may not show until the plant is 1.8 m (6 ft) high when the leaves will turn yellow and drop, and the bush tilts over because its anchorage is weak. Scrape around the base of the stem and feel for a thick smooth plate of hard wood blocking the supply channels and spread of the roots. The bush can be left tilted over to encourage suckers to grow from the roots, so bypassing the plate and, if they do, the old top can be cut off. This will only be effective if the camellia is not a grafted plant. Normally only new varieties and foreign plants are grafted.

I am often asked if a large plant can be moved and the answer is usually 'yes'. In most of Britain the top soil is only a spit deep and most of the fibrous roots are in it with an occasional thick anchor root, as distinct from the deep pumice soils of New Zealand where the majority of roots go far down.

So, assume that the rootball extends a little beyond the spread of foliage and, there, cut down with the spade in a circle. If a mechanical digger can be obtained, the whole plant can be dug up and carried in its shovel to the new site or put on a thick polythene sheet for transport on a vehicle. Have its new hole larger than required and fill in with extra peat in the soil. If lifting by hand, first dig a trench out round the rootball, then undercut the plant at the spade's depth or a little less, tilt it up and slip under it the wrapper of a big peat bale. Ease the whole plant on to this and it can be dragged to its new hole.

If in doubt about the fibrous nature of the roots cut around the plant in the spring and move it in the autumn. If a good rootball is not retained prune half the branches out to reduce the demand on the roots for water.

PRUNING AND TRAINING

Pruning is done regularly in the USA to space apart the branches in order to get show flowers. In New Zealand it is done to contain exuberant growth and to reduce the lodgement of pests in the centre of the bush. In Britain it occurs as a question 'Can I cut my camellia?' When one looks at the camellias in the long greenhouse at Eaton Hall in Cheshire and realizes that at one time the whole house was filled with a tangle blocking it completely, and then one gazes at the sheer perfection of growth, flowers and training today, the answer can only be 'yes' (Fig. 4). Bear in mind that the large pink flowers in the photograph are those of *Camellia reticulata* 'Capt. Rawes', and another question is answered, or a falsehood corrected, for it is often said that 'retics' cannot be pruned. So you can prune for shape, or cut flowers for a party, preferably cutting back to a side-shoot. You can also cut an old camellia on its own roots right to the ground and it will rejuvenate itself in a year or two (Fig. 5).

Camellias are used in Spain or Portugal for hedges and topiary. Bushes

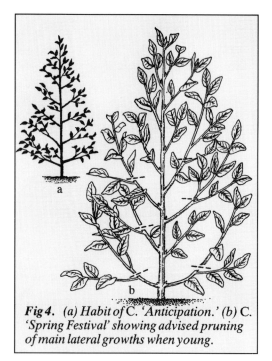

Fig 4. *(a) Habit of C. 'Anticipation.' (b) C. 'Spring Festival' showing advised pruning of main lateral growths when young.*

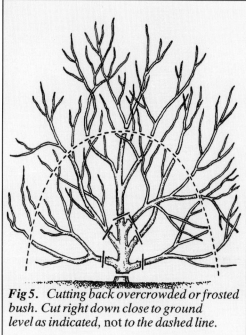

Fig 5. *Cutting back overcrowded or frosted bush. Cut right down close to ground level as indicated,* not *to the dashed line.*

should be clipped in late winter or just *before* flowering is over and new growth has begun.

For covering walls, either varieties specially adapted for that, such as 'Francie L' or 'Royalty', are best. So often one sees old *japonica* plants grown out 0.5 m (1½ft) or more from the wall, blocking the opening of windows and doors. To prevent this pruning or clipping must be pretty ruthless and done annually without fail.

In the old days when camellias were priced and sold by height, the nurseries often sent them out with single stems. Nowadays most plants, except for the 23–30 cm (9–12 in) plants, which should never be put on the market, are sold

with a decent set of lateral branches, starting out 15 cm (6 in) above the compost, and a strong leading shoot. In the nursery this framework is achieved not by pruning but by pinching out the softer tips of the appropriate shoots between finger and thumb. Anyone can do this with their own camellia indoors or out. From the Midlands northwards it is advisable to choose a plant not less than 60 cm (2 ft) high.

When training a new plant on a wall the structure of the branches will be something like the diagram which illustrates where the cut should be made when pruning in spring to encourage a lateral branch to train in and flower next year (Fig. 6).

CULTIVATION OUTDOORS

Mulching and feeding are the essentials. A mulch is a layer of soft organic material to simulate the leaf fall in a forest. It can be leafmould or peat but not soil which should never be spread over the roots of camellias.

Medium-grade sphagnum peat has a habit of caking and letting moisture out, instead of keeping it in which is a function of the mulch. This can now be overcome by spreading a top layer of ground fir bark or wood chippings. If this is done watch out for honey fungus and double the amount of nitrogen put on in spring. This is because the bacteria which attack the top mulch use up the nitrogen in the soil in order to do so.

Where the soil is unsuitable camellias can still be grown outdoors. If the existing soil is acid or neutral but otherwise unusable a raised bed can be built up using ordinary walling materials, without limestone or mortar, or peat blocks can be used. The bed should be at least 0.6m (2ft) deep and a camellia will last a long time in a bed a metre (3¼ft) square (Fig. 7a).

Where the soil formation is alkaline such a raised bed can be lined with a polythene sheet, obtainable from a builders' merchant, making drainage holes in the bottom covered by a thick layer of gravel or polystyrene. Or, if there is no danger of water seeping in, the bed can be excavated and lined (Fig. 7b).

Where all else fails, camellias can be cultivated very successfully in pots or tubs filled with ericaceous or acid com-post. John Innes compost contains chalk and is unsuitable. John Innes 'A' is good, if obtainable. Once established, camellias in containers will require feeding and the best way is to add a liquid feed to the water when watering between mid-spring and late summer but *not* in the dormant season. The absolute essential is to ensure that the roots do not get frozen. Move the containers to safety, or box them in with polystyrene or straw or sawdust, any good insulator. Many a camellia has come through a hard winter unprotected and looked fine in early spring, but suddenly dead a month later when the sun has gained power. The water-pump below (the roots) has failed.

Keep camellias labelled or recorded in a safe place. Memory fades and the day will come when you want advice, or

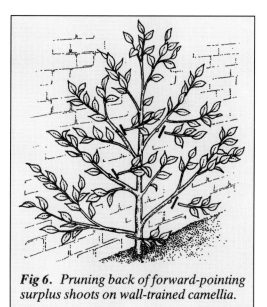

Fig 6. *Pruning back of forward-pointing surplus shoots on wall-trained camellia.*

to give a plant to a friend and the name will be essential.

Watering must be thought about during a spell of dry weather, for the mulch will not give complete security from drought to a young plant which has a very limited root spread. Use rain water if available but if the soil is acid, and preparation has been correctly carried out, tap water can be safely used for many weeks. A good soaking once a week is better than fiddling with a water can with a rose on it, although camellias do like damping over.

Camellias respond to feeding annually but many gardeners are afraid to feed them. The purpose of feeding is to promote healthy growth: those glossy leaves, the formation of flower buds and the hardiness to get them through the winter and into flower in spring. Most soils contain enough of the trace elements such as copper, manganese, molybdenum and iron which are needed for the plant's functioning and the interaction and control of the main elements, nitrogen, phosphorus, potassium, calcium and magnesium. Calcium has already been mentioned and for camellias it is, practically, a trace element.

Most complete fertilizers are sold with stated percentage contents of N for nitrogen, P for phosphoric acid and K for potassium: one or two include magnesium and trace elements and the label may say whether the nitrogen is in the form of ammonia or nitrate. If this sounds too complicated buy a labelled rhododendron and azalea fertilizer and put it on in early spring as recom-

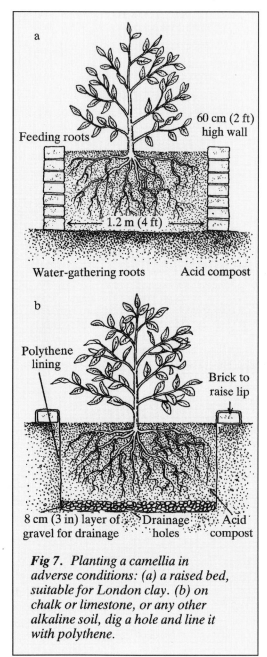

Fig 7. Planting a camellia in adverse conditions: (a) a raised bed, suitable for London clay. (b) on chalk or limestone, or any other alkaline soil, dig a hole and line it with polythene.

mended! I use Vitax Rhododendron and Azalea Fertilizer.

The sap of camellias, like rhododendrons, must be acid. Hence the need for acid soil and the wisdom in using fertilizers having an acid reaction. The acidic fertilizers contain ammonium nitrogen (sold separately as sulphate of ammonia); phosphorus is contained in superphosphate (which again supplies calcium), and ammonium phosphate; potassium in sulphate of potash and magnesium in the sulphate (Epsom salts) and oxide forms.

Unsuitable fertilizers are Nitro-chalk, or other nitrate compounds, wood ashes, bone meal and basic slag.

Nitrogen is for growth, potassium promotes the manufacture of food in healthy leaves, phosphate is for healthy roots and flowers and, working in harness with potash and magnesium, fosters ripening and hardiness.

The degree of hardiness of the individual plant depends largely on the time that growth starts to slow down before the winter, so allowing the wood and flower buds to ripen properly. Therefore, nitrogen, which stimulates growth, should be given early in the year and it is conveniently done with a dressing of a compound fertilizer in early spring when rain should wash it down among the roots. Most of the compound fertilizers have an analysis around 7% N, 7% P and 7% K and this does not contain enough nitrogen for a camellia so an additional dressing of 32g per m^2 (1 oz per sq yd) of sulphate of ammonia should be put on in mid-spring. It is very soluble and will burn any foliage it falls

on. If a mulch of fir bark or chippings has been put on, double this top-dressing. If by mid-summer flower buds are not apparent a top-dressing of superphosphate and of Epsom salts, each at 32g per m^2 (1oz per sq yd), may then promote them but there must be enough nitrogen left from the spring to enable the superphosphate to work safely.

Fertilizers should never be put on dry soil. During a period of not too heavy rainfall is the best time.

Follow this advice and an iron tonic should not be required or desirable.

There are some weeds worth mentioning. They can create havoc in a camellia. The worst is sycamore seedlings which blow into the middle of the bush. By the time the tops are visible among the camellia branches they cannot be pulled out and have to be cut down and the cut stump painted with a brushwood killer in diesel oil or covered with crystals of ammonium sulphamate. Ash, with its winged keys is nearly as bad. Brambles are the devil. A minute seedling appears right by the main stem and clambers up through the branches of the camellia and soon the tip of every branch has taken root. Ivy is another insidious invader. The seeds have been excreted by blackbirds or thrushes. Fieldfares will deposit yew seeds the same way. The only answer is eternal vigilance, an annual inspection inside the bush to remove seedlings in their first season either by hand directly or the use of a Dutch type hoe which cuts on the pull as well as the push.

Outside weeds can be prevented by using the weedkiller simazine as directed, at half strength in late winter and mid-summer.

The removal of dead flowers is known as grooming. Many of the × *williamsii* hybrids and the species, the reticulatas and a few japonicas will drop their dead flowers. Faced with a multitude of dead flowers on a hedge of 'Tiptoe' I take a long-handled dung-fork, insert it carefully in the bush and shake it vigorously. It leaves a minority to be picked by hand.

CULTIVATION IN GREENHOUSES

Few plants can outdo a camellia in a greenhouse or polythene tunnel. The form of the flowers may be different from those outdoors, some better, like 'Leonard Messel', some not so good, like 'Bob Hope', but the whites and pale pinks will attain greater size and perfection and last longer. The choice is greater too.

The fragrance of *Camellia oleifera* is sensed at a distance outdoors but the scents of the species *C. kissii* and *C. grijsii* and its form *yuhsienensis*, *C. lutchuensis* and its progeny, 'Fragrant Pink', *C. fraterna* and its hybrid 'Tiny Princess', the 'Girls', already mentioned in 'Choosing the Best' and *C. japonica* 'Kramer's Supreme', are only spread and enjoyed under cover when the day temperature rises to 15.5°C (60°F). By and large these, the *reticulata* and the *japonica* camellias are the choice for a greenhouse, the × *williamsii* for outdoors.

For the sub-tropical species, including the yellow *Camellia chrysantha* and *C.*

euphlebia, a regular heating system will be necessary but otherwise a reserve heater for very cold spells will be enough. Calor gas is safer than electricity. No power cuts. Flowers will last longer and stay perfect at a low temperature, 4–5°C (40°F), but when the flowers are over and the bushes in growth the temperature may rise to 26°C (80°F). It is then that the humidity must be kept up by shading and by damping over during the day with a sprinkler or hosepipe. The ventilation should be open at all times except in frosty or very windy weather.

Camellias planted in a greenhouse will, inevitably, be planted too closely: one must have this and that, and that new one is irresistible! Immediately after flowering they should be worked over, cutting branches back to side shoots nearer the main stem and thinning out where necessary. They can be trained like cordon gooseberries to restrict them or let go and then cut down at intervals of a few years, probably the best way for the species mentioned.

In pots camellias will probably need to be moved on into a larger size every other year until the final stage is reached. After several years in its last container the plant will no longer be maintainable without action. Take it in time. Do not wait until the buds have dropped and the leaves are yellow and falling. Take the green plant in winter out of its large pot or tub, cut half its rootball off, put it back in the container and fill with fresh compost. At the same time thin out the branches by half. If that succeeds, and the plant shows by its leaf growth and flowers that it is rejuvenated, cut the other half of the rootball off two years after the first. Until the roots have spread into the new compost feed lightly when watering and do not overwater.

Pots are not crocked nowadays but filled with compost to about 2.5 cm (1 in) from the top to allow for watering. In order to avoid unsightly splashing it's worth covering the compost with pebbles.

Potted this way a plant can be stood on capillary matting and is able to take up water from below while you are absent from home.

It is normal to move camellias in pots out of the greenhouse to enable a summer crop to be grown in it. They come into tender growth very early in a greenhouse and this is prone to frost damage. Rather wait until early summer or rig up a shelter.

If the pots are safe from frost they can be left out in a sheltered partly shaded place until re-housing after a chrysanthemum crop.

DISEASES

Camellias are not plagued by any disease so persistent as black spot of roses, or apple scab nor any pest so regular and damaging as carrot root-fly or cabbage caterpillars, but they are not immune from trouble and the worst hide behind a screen of sooty mould, at once revealing and deceiving. It tells you that trouble is there but misleads you on to the wrong track. This section of the chapter is intended to identify the trouble and to specify the method of dealing with it.

□ LEAF MOTTLE VIRUS

The commonest disease is called leaf mottle virus, which is endemic in most old Japanese and Chinese camellias which have been propagated vegetatively for many years. It is wise to assume that any camellia with a Japanese or Chinese name is infected. Some show yellow mottling on the leaves or they may be wholly yellow on some branches. Others may have only one yellow spot on a fully grown bush. Others again may be carriers without exhibiting any visual symptoms. The infection is distributed in two ways – firstly by knife, as in grafting, and secondly by sap-sucking insects – aphids or scale insects.

Once the disease is within the plant it cannot yet be removed. Work is being done on its elimination, so far without complete success. Within the plant the virus breaks down the cells. In the flowers it causes white blotching. Any name with the three letters 'var' after it indicates that the virus has been introduced deliberately, a not very sensible American ploy. Striped flowers are not usually infected. Whole branches with yellow leaves can be greened up by a heavy dose of sulphate of ammonia. The virus reduces the quality of flowers a little but, otherwise, does little harm.

There are thought to be several forms of the virus, one of which reduces the size of the leaves and peppers them with silvery specks and flecks. This is dangerous and a bush infected in this way should be burnt.

There are two other types of yellowing which are not viroid. One is the pale yellow edging of some leaves of × *williamsii* hybrids. This is thought to be due to excessive changes of temperature between day and night. The other is simple variegation, notably in the form of *Camellia* × *williamsii* 'Mary Christian' called 'Golden Spangles' and in the Japanese chimaeras called 'Benten' and 'Reigyoku', the first silver, the second gold, each with little red flowers.

☐ CAMELLIA LEAF-GALL

An odd disease, more frequent in recent years, is camellia leaf-gall (*Exobasidium camelliae*) which causes a repulsive, white, jelly-like enlargement of a leaf or flower. It is usually sufficient to cut off the infected part of the plant and burn it. If it recurs, spray with mancozeb or copper fungicide.

☐ LEAF SPOT

If a greenhouse or, more likely, a polythene tunnel is allowed to get very hot without ventilation two diseases may occur: one is leaf spot (*Pestalotiopsis guepini*) which shows as grey or brown spots on the leaves, especially if shoots from such a source are used for cuttings. They may be given a benomyl drench.

☐ STEM WILT

The second disease is stem wilt (*Glomerella cingulata*) which causes stems to bend over and, if severely infected, to die. I have seen it only on *reticulata* camellias in Britain but it can be very harmful in hotter countries such as Australia and the USA. It should not appear outdoors in Britain nor, with good under cover ventilation.

☐ HONEY FUNGUS

Honey fungus (*Armillaria mellea*) does attack camellias. In my case the fungus fed on a beech stump and, when it had removed all the lignin, spread out among a lot of camellias planted closely on trial. The honey-coloured toadstools, from which it gets its name, are not significant, nor are the thick long bootlaces or rhizomorphs by which it travels. It is the fans of fine rhizophores with the black changing to chestnut brown, and the tips sharp and piercing, which attack and eat away the roots. In a large Cornish garden, copper carbonate has been used in the past to control this fungus and root-rotting *Phytophthora cinnamomi* with complete success.

A camellia attacked by honey fungus shows it by the yellowing of drooping leaves and, in advanced attacks, by a loss of anchorage as the roots are destroyed. The rhizomorphs will be found about 13 cm below the soil surface.

PESTS

☐ APHIDS

The two significant pests, aphids and scale insects, have the same visual symptoms of their presence – sooty mould which grows on the surface of the leaf below another one being attacked by

Opposite: *The Corridor Greenhouse at Eaton Hall, Cheshire, home of the Duke of Westminster, was built in 1840. The pink camellia in the foreground is C. j. 'Elegans'.*

one of these pests on the undersurface of the leaves above. In each case the insect is sucking the sap out. As it sucks in the sap it excretes a sugary liquid, or honey dew, on to the surface of the leaf below where the sooty mould lives on it purely as a scavenger or opportunist.

Young camellia plants in early soft growth in a greenhouse, frame or tunnel, may be attacked by large green aphids. It is essential to kill them immediately for they are the carriers of leaf mottle virus. Later, brown aphids in summer or autumn outdoors and at any time under glass may swarm on to the undersides of the young leaves, curling them up.

Under glass prevention is by the use of suspended vaporizing strips and control indoors and out is by spraying with pirimicarb, malathion or dimethoate.

□ SCALE INSECTS

Scale insects always seem to find camellias in the end. There are two common types: the first is the cushion scale, which looks like small wads of cotton wool on the undersides of the leaves, mostly near the edges. On young plants they can be squeezed off by hand. The second is the soft scale which is less noticeable but a worse pest because it is small and breeds more quickly. It has a smooth case about 4mm (3/16in) long, half as wide, yellow brown, fixed to the under-surface of the leaves, often along the mid-rib or the edge, and on the stems of young growths.

The insects live and feed under the white wool or the cases. In late spring and early summer, and again in early autumn, the young insects or crawlers emerge and move up the stems and the adults move up to younger leaves. These are the times to spray to wet thoroughly the stems and undersides of the leaves with malathion or a permethrin spray. It will take at least two sprayings to be effective and it will be wise to spray again the following late spring.

□ VINE WEEVILS

Vine weevils (*Otiorrhynchus sulcatus*) may be a pest under glass. If there is litter about, the black long-snouted adults will hide under it – leaves, paper, pots, boxes, sacking, straw etc. At night they emerge to feed and lay eggs. All are female and each can lay in excess of 500 eggs. If laid in the compost of potted plants they hatch out under it and develop into white grubs with brown heads which eat the roots away and girdle the stem. The presence of the weevil is very often revealed by the notches it cuts out when feeding on the edges of the leaves. They are attracted to the greenhouse if it has primulas in it.

In a small greenhouse the adult can be collected at night by torchlight and destroyed. The larvae can be controlled by drenching all pots in the house with a gamma-HCH solution. Adults can also be killed by dusts of gamma-HCH or carbaryl. A new biological control, using an eelworm to kill the grubs, may shortly be available.

□ BIRDS

Single and semi-double camellias have much nectar in the centre of their flowers. Birds, particularly blue tits in Britain, will damage the petals to get at the nectar at any time before the nesting period. A bird-repellent spray should be used on the first two fine days in a row when there are open flowers. I have found a spray based on quassia ineffective and one based on an aluminium compound successful.

□ **MAMMALS**
In snow, especially if the camellias are in grass, mice may girdle the main stem and kill the plant. In hard weather the grey squirrel may remove flower buds.

DISORDERS

□ **CORKY SCAB**
Corky scab or oedema shows as linear brown excrescences on one or both surfaces of the leaf. The cause is unknown but it is thought to be a physiological reaction to continuous humid conditions in the air and/or the soil. Keeping a buoyant atmosphere under glass and thinning the branches to admit air outdoors may help. Removing the leaves alone makes it worse.

□ **BALLING**
Balling occurs more frequently in hotter climates. I saw it once only – in the spring of 1984, when the days were very hot indeed, associated with a long spell of drying east winds and cold nights. The outer petals of the swelling buds could not unfold, and split away at the base of the flower, which could not open. Such flowers should be taken off immediately.

To summarize, some diagnostic notes:

Yellow leaves: mostly older ones, sometimes with the veins staying green indicate lack of water or fertilizer or both, because feed is taken up only in solution. Yellow and brown blotches between the veins indicate alkaline soil.

Mottled yellow leaves with sometimes a branch wholly yellow – leaf mottle virus.

A faint *yellow edge to the leaf*. A harmless physiological reaction of × *williamsii* camellias.

Brown shading on leaf surfaces, showing on the curved part – inadequate water and humus and a hot position.

Brown blisters through the leaf. Outdoors, sun scorch due to exposure to burning sunlight. Indoors, lack of ventilation, shading and humidity. Leaf spot looks similar but occurs in excessive damp heat.

Leaves brown-edged with a pale yellowing surface – chemical imbalance; lime accessible to roots; excessive feed; animal manure; spreading soil over roots. With leaf-drop under glass – feeding too late in the year or too heavily; overwatering.

Purplish brown patches on the leaves in spring/autumn may be frost damage.

White powder along the leaf edges – excessive salts from chemicals in soil or in water.

Black sooty deposits – see aphids and scale insects.

Brown warty excrescences – corky scab.

Grey-green encrustation under trees – harmless algae on upper leaf surface.

CHAPTER FIVE

PROPAGATION

This final chapter is divided into four sections: raising plants from seeds, plants from cuttings, grafting, and breeding new camellias. None of these is difficult; in fact a head gardener in Cornwall, allegedly retired, reckons camellia cuttings are too easy and prefers the challenge of supplying most of Britain's lapagerias!

The early settlers in New Zealand had no greenhouses or modern gadgetry. Their cuttings were simply stuck in the open ground in a plot which suited them. True, there is no more ideal climate. It is said that a camellia cutting dropped on the pavement in New Plymouth will root there!

Grafting was practised in China centuries ago, using as stocks varieties found to root easily or seedlings of local species. Unfortunately, leaf-mottle virus, of which no-one knows the origin, has been long established in China and Japan and there is no surer way of transmitting it than by grafting on an infected understock, or by the ancient practice of inarching – discarded in the west as recently as 1930.

It was thought to be the only means of increasing varieties of *C. reticulata*. A stock plant in a pot was perched up among the branches of the chosen bush in a greenhouse and the surface pared off a part of the stem of the stock and of a conveniently situated branch of the variety, the two cut surfaces brought together and tied securely and kept in a humid atmosphere until the join was established well enough to permit the severance of the parent branch and the top of the stock. Today, by skill or science, or the alchemy of a rooting chemical, we take cuttings and they grow.

RAISING CAMELLIAS FROM SEEDS

In a good year, greenish-brown, apple-like fruits may be found on mature bushes. *Camellia japonica* 'Adolphe Audusson' is a fraud – the fruits are always empty. The fertile fruits will ripen in the autumn and should be harvested before they begin to split. Once the seed is brown they are ripe enough. If left too long they will all drop very smartly one night and the seed roll out and be lost. The seeds are about the size of peanuts and should be sown straight away or stored dry in a refrigerator, not a freezer, until early spring. Then put them among chopped sphagnum moss. If you can find it, it is much the best because it holds just the right amount of moisture and has antiseptic properties. Put moss – or peat if you cannot get moss – and seeds in a polythene bag and put it in the clothes – airing cupboard.

In six to eight weeks roots should be visible. Open the bag and, if the roots are 8cm (3in) long, carefully separate out the seedlings, cut off one third of the roots, and pot them up in 8cm (3in) pots in an ericaceous compost, just covering the seed. It takes quite a while for a shoot to push up.

Keep moist but do not over-water. Above all keep clear of mice by putting the pots in a tray on glass jars, or some other way.

When the shoots expand into leaves grow on like potted rooted cuttings. Grow on in pots until flowering – up to five years.

PLANTS FROM CUTTINGS

Cuttings of most camellias root readily, including *reticulata* camellias. A few, such as 'Augusto L'Gouveia Pinto', will root but refuse to grow away and are, therefore, often grafted. In Australia, the prevalence of a disease makes it desirable to graft on a disease-resistant stock, the *sasanqua* 'Kanjiro', but this is not a problem in Europe. The use of cuttings eliminates the hazard of the stock growing, unobserved, later in life, so raising the problem, brought to me, of the camellia with two different flowers!

To ensure success cuttings should be put into a propagator or bed which has bottom heat and a covering which enables a saturated atmosphere to be maintained. Commercially, heat is supplied by electric heating cables, or small-bore water pipes, controlled by a thermostat to keep the rooting medium at 20°C (70°F). The saturated atmosphere used to be maintained by mist nozzles with electrical controls. Now it is done on a large scale by fogging devices or, more cheaply, by covering the beds with ordinary or 'bubble' polythene sheets. For the amateur there is a choice of self-contained mist propagators requiring connections to a water pipe and electricity, or simply heated propagating cases.

In mid- to late summer the wood of camellia shoots hardens and the bush has a resting period before it either makes flower buds or moves into secondary growth. In Britain this is late mid-summer. Cuttings can be taken then. It is a time of year when the heat in a greenhouse will keep the temperature of the propagator up without using much electricity.

Cuttings can continue to be taken until the end of winter.

The first to be ready will be *reticulata* camellias. Most people graft these but that is not necessary. The secret of success, as with magnolias, is to root them in pots so that there is no root disturbance later and the rooted cutting can, simply, be potted on in early summer or late spring.

The form of the cutting is the same throughout but with a preference for tip cuttings (Fig. 8*a*). These are simply the ends of the young shoots with two or three axillary leaves and buds and the tip bud with its leaf or twin leaves. Cut or pull off the bottom leaf or two leaves and, with a sharp knife, shave off a 2.5 cm (1 in) sliver of stem from the side opposite the basal bud. If a long shoot of *japonica*, × *williamsii* and species camellias has been cut from the bush, cuttings may be made below the terminal cutting (Fig. 8*b*). If a strong shoot with stout buds grows on a particularly desirable bush, bud cuttings can be made of each bud with its leaf and short intermediate length of stem (Fig. 8*c*). These will take a year longer to grow into a plant of saleable size.

The cuttings are dipped in a hormone rooting powder or liquid. It is not necessary to cut the leaves in half before inserting the cuttings.

Cuttings are rooted in a mixture of 75% peat and 25% grit. Sharp grit can be bought graded for this purpose but there are alternative manufactured products – horticultural (not builders') vermiculite, perlite, and polystyrene granules.

Prepare the chosen mixture, wet it well and fill the bed of the propagator without pressing it down. If only camellias are to fill it, simply stick the cuttings in. If other plants are to be rooted with them, it is better to root them all in small pots so that they can be taken out as they are ready. After inserting the

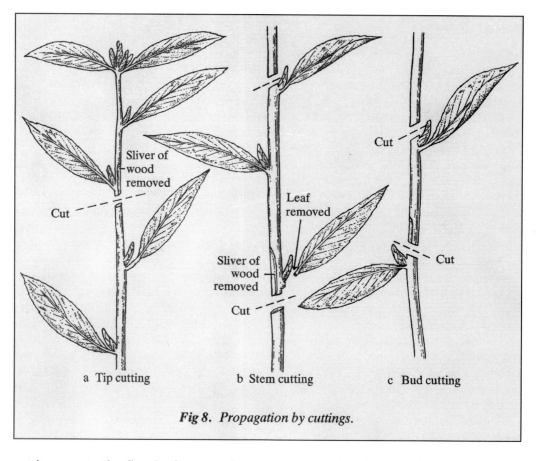

Fig 8. Propagation by cuttings.

cuttings up to the first leaf, water them in and put the lid of the propagator on or cover with polythene so that moisture condenses on the underside of it. If in a propagator with a mist unit, simply turn on the water and electricity and check that the latter is activating the mist at the right intervals to keep the leaves damp but not drowned. Cuttings should root in six to twelve weeks when the mist can be turned off or the polythene opened up to let air in and wean the cuttings to an ordinary regime of growth

and watering. Do not be worried if × *williamsii* cuttings come into flower. Let them be, but take away dead flowers. On a large scale whole-house fogging can be used instead of mist nozzles or polythene.

There is a new development upon which I dare not elaborate because changes are taking place in methods and constituents. This is the use of slow-release fertilizers in the cutting bed. Slow-release fertilizers are most valuable in commercial production of camellias. They are pellets containing fertilizer, the release of which is regulated by the formulation of the pellets. This is a modern development in which the original vendor is competing with another fertilizer manufacturer and it is unsafe to give a detailed assessment. This year one works well; the next year the other is better. All I dare recommend is a study of the literature where the slow-release fertilizers are sold. They are a great aid in nursery practice from the cutting stage onwards.

Cuttings taken in late summer can be potted into 8 cm (3 in) pots in late winter or early spring. Those taken in late autumn or winter can wait until late spring or early summer. Keep them in a shaded greenhouse or frame. Once they are established, open all the ventilators and doors as often as possible and give them a chance to become hardy.

The cuttings of one year will pass the winter rooting and being potted up, stay under glass for one growing season, be potted on into the next size pot during the next autumn or winter and wait under glass for all danger of frost to be past in the following spring and then, as strong well-branched plants be plunged outdoors in sawdust, sand or soil in a partly shaded place.

They can be fed either by incorporating slow-release fertilizers in the compost when potting on, by feeding with a rhododendron and azalea fertilizer put on the compost surface in spring or by adding a liquid feed to the water when watering during the growing season, stopping in late summer. If the dry feed is given ensure that the compost in the pot is wet before putting it on the surface and water it in.

In the autumn these plants should be 45–60 cm (18–24 in) high and fit to be planted in the south of England. From the Midlands northwards another year's growth, to get a plant with more hard wood and height, is advisable.

GRAFTING

Grafting does gain one year of growth but in Britain it is used, only infrequently, for new camellias and to increase stock more quickly before settling down to cuttings. In Australia, cutting grafts to unite the scion of the variety to a cutting of *sasanqua* 'Kanjiro' is used to confer to the variety the resistance of the stock to *Botrytis cinnamomea*, a disease which is not normally a trouble in Britain where the stocks are either seedlings or *japonica* camellias or surplus plants. Seedlings are safe but any camellia with a Chinese or Japanese name will almost certainly have leaf mottle virus which will be transmitted to the scion with appalling visual consequences.

Grafting is done in late winter, just before the sap rises. Select root stocks with stems 1.2 cm (½ in) thick or more at 8 cm (3 in) above the compost level.

The first step is to dry out the plant until the compost in the pot just needs watering. Next cut off the top of the stock about 8 cm (3 in) from the roots, using secateurs, and then trim the cut with a sharp knife. Hold the knife over the centre of the cut and press it down to split the stock. If it is a larger stock and too tough for this take an old thin table knife and tap it gently with a hammer to make the split. Cut a scion, just like a cutting but from the middle or base of a strong firm young growth and, instead of cutting a sliver off it, use a very sharp knife to trim it into a long wedge thin enough to fit tightly into the split but firm enough not to fray. Push the wedge in one side of the split so that the bark of both stock and scion meet each other and stay put. If the stock is a thicker one it may be necessary to hold the cut open by pushing in a screw-driver to hold it while the scion is being inserted. Tie the stock round with raffia or grafting tape. It need not be waxed over but it is neater to do so, or a wad of sphagnum moss can be put over the cuts (Fig. 9).

Put a layer of damp sand over the compost and press down into it the rim of an inverted plastic or glass jar to shut out air and retain moisture. Put in a shaded place in the greenhouse.

When there are signs of growth a little water may be given but only a little. At the same time insert a finger through the sand under the rim of the jar to let in a little air.

When the growth looks firm and reliable ease up the jar and on a dull day take it off. If the growth wilts put it back on and wean it a little longer keeping it shaded. As soon as the jar is off greenfly will appear and a pyrethrum spray should be used to kill them. So will side shoots from the stock and they must be rubbed or cut off.

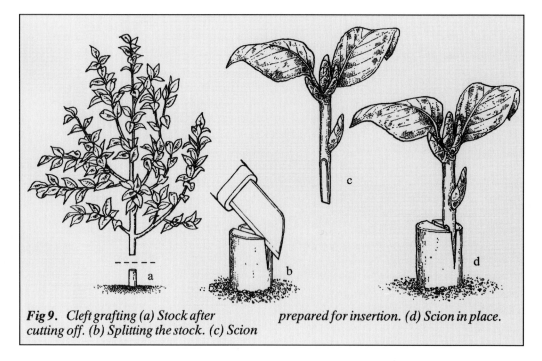

Fig 9. *Cleft grafting (a) Stock after cutting off. (b) Splitting the stock. (c) Scion prepared for insertion. (d) Scion in place.*

Having used a rootstock which has a dry and restricted root system, as soon as the scion is growing away and obviously firmly established, pot the plant on into a larger pot, grow it on and let it harden off before winter.

BREEDING NEW CAMELLIAS

□ SIZE

A well-known New Zealand nursery-man, Nevill Haydon, says that most of his requests are not for particular colours or forms of flower, but simply for a camellia which will not exceed 1.2–1.5 m (4–5 ft) in height, in other words an attractive plant that fits neatly in a small front garden without hogging all the space.

I can think of only one which lays any claim to such a character – 'Akashiren', or 'Hassaku', a single red, whose entitlement to be called 'The Dwarf', is probably related more to slow growth than final size.

The tea plant is often illustrated as bushes on hillside terraces, with Chinese or Indian women standing head and shoulders above them. Only the plucking of the shoots prevents these bushes from becoming trees.

There are some species, such as _C. rosaeflora_, which make low bushes and are now being exploited by plant breeders, but this species is not hardy in Britain. In theory there is no reason why short bushy camellias in many varieties should not be bred but it would take a long time to raise the varieties of form and colour now available in larger bushes, which can be limited only by pruning.

□ SPORTS

Sports are not bred: they are variations which occur on a part of a plant by chance. One flower or branch may change colour and, if it is the first occurrence of the change, the owner may be the fortunate possessor of a new camellia without any effort on his or her part beyond taking a shoot from the changed branch, rooting it as a cutting, and bringing it into flower to prove its stability. This is not always so easy as it seems. In the case of 'Little Bit' the change is a fairly stable one, and although 'Lady Vansittart' may have five different blooms on one bush, its sport 'Yours Truly' is fairly stable. Not so 'Betty Sheffield Supreme', a beautiful pink and white peony from which 14 sports have been named. The happy nuseryman may think he is selling 'Betty Sheffield Supreme' until a customer tells him he has been sent a lovely white, after which every plant has to be flowered before it can be sold. (That happened!)

The most successful sporting camellia is 'Elegans', first sold by Chandler in London in 1831. Along with the offspring from its sports, it is still providing American nurserymen with new and worthy camellias. 'Elegans Champagne' reached the market in 1975.

□ HYBRIDIZING

To the botanical purist this may mean breeding from two different species but the dictionary adds 'or varieties'.

In Australia and New Zealand, where self-sown seedlings abound, many new registrations are of chance seedlings which the garden owner has grown on to flower with success. In Britain this may happen in a small way in a good season or in the south west. The low-growing 'Taroan', for instance, seeds freely, and although many of its seedlings come true or very similar to the parent a new hybrid may occur. It is certainly worth sowing the seeds.

The majority of new camellias are of amateur origin.

SELECTING THE PARENTS

In *Camellia Nomenclature* the first name in the parentage of a hybrid is that of the seed parent and there is some guidance in those names and the performance of the progeny.

Avoid using a × *williamsii* hybrid as a seed parent for a cross with a *japonica*. The progeny is likely to be difficult to flower at a normal age for commercial production.

The × *williamsii* hybrids lack reds and whites. It is tempting to use the dark red *C. japonica* 'Fuyajo' as a pollen parent. It conveys a lack of hardiness but 'Konron-koku' is hardier and may be better.

The species *C. cuspidata* has a good but too small record as a parent, with 'Spring Festival' the recent notable example of achievement. The success of the hybrid 'Cornish Spring' – *cuspidata* × *japonica* 'Rosea Simplex' – was not followed up. Opportunity beckons!

Camellias with flowers that shatter have been discarded in the USA because of a petal blight which is spread by the fallen petals. This disease is not present in Australia, New Zealand, and Europe where flowers that shatter when over are most desirable because they save grooming and enhance the appearance of the bush e.g. *C.* × *williamsii* 'Charles Colbert'.

More camellias with the growth habit of 'Anticipation' and different colours are highly desirable.

POLLINATION

Pollination is the process of transferring pollen from one flower to the stigma of another to obtain seeds. In Britain it has to be done in a greenhouse if the requisite 15°C (59°F) is to be maintained. It can be done locally by means of an electric light bulb in a polythene bag or similar device. Timing the heating may be necessary to get seed and pollen parents in flower at the same time. It is the seed parent which requires the heating.

Each flower has a central ovary, or seed vessel, surrounded by stamens ending in the male pollen-bearing anthers. The ovary has a single style, or short stalk, ending in three or five arms, or it may have three or more separate styles. Styles and anthers are lacking in formal double varieties but may be induced to grow by heating the plants in a greenhouse.

When the flower of the seed parent begins to open, cut away the anthers with a pair of scissors to prevent self-fertilization. Within three days of the flower opening, the stigmas become moist and ready to receive pollen. Pollen can be brushed on with a camel's hair brush or a ripe anther used to touch each stigma gently. Segregate the female flower from alien pollen by enclosing it in a polythene bag or insect-proof cage. Label the stem with data of the time and nature of the cross. If the pollination is successful, the fruit will look like a small apple and split open in early autumn. The seed can be harvested when brown before it is shed.

Grow the seedlings on in a greenhouse, potting on when necessary, and root and label cuttings as soon as they are available. They may flower before the more vigorous parent plant which can be grown on outdoors. Full flowering may take five to ten years.

APPENDIX

The International Camellia Society, founded in 1962, is the international registration authority for camellias organized with directors in twelve regions of the world. The executive moves from region to region every three years in accordance with the elections of the president and in 1990 is in the USA.

A journal is published annually and an international congress is held biennially. In Britain a gathering is organized each spring to visit gardens and see camellias in flower.

Each region has a membership representative who collects subscriptions and may prepare and send out a newsletter once or twice a year. For the United Kingdom the secretary is Mrs. M. E. Scott-Moncrieff, Buff Wardour, Tisbury, Salisbury, Wilts., SP3 6RE; and for the Channel Islands, Eire and other European countries, Mrs. Ann Bushell, Lower Hall, Rue de la Pompe, Augres, Trinity, Jersey, Channel Islands.

In Britain, trials of camellias are sponsored in Staffordshire, Harlow Car near Harrogate, Edinburgh and Belfast and members are involved with the National Collection at Mt. Edgcumbe in Cornwall.

The American Camellia Society, organized in 1945, is based at Fort Valley, Georgia and issues a quarterly journal largely concerned with membership and flower shows. Its year book covers research, history, technical matters and the year's registrations of new camellias. It is linked with Britain through Mrs. M. G. Reynolds of Westward, Le Marquanderie, St. Brelade, Jersey, Channel Islands, who acts as agent for membership.

The New Zealand Camellia Society was founded in 1958 and has branches throughout both islands. It is active in research, assessing new camellias, organizing shows and publishing four issues each year of the New Zealand Camellia Bulletin, much of which is relevant to Britain, especially the information about new varieties. The secretary at present is Mr. G. L. Warsaw at Box 204, Wanganui, North Island.

The Southern California Camellia Society is prominent in the camellia world through its biennial publication of *Camellia Nomenclature* which, since the Historical Edition of 1984, publishes the name and descriptions of new camellias and others in general cultivation today. It also has a quarterly *Camellia Review*. The address is Southern Camellia Society, 695 Winston Avenue, San Marino, CA 91108, USA.

The Royal Horticultural Society has a Rhododendron and Camellia Group, and a committee which judges camellias submitted for awards and selects for trial at Wisley.

INDEX

ACKNOWLEDGEMENTS

The publishers gratefully acknowledge the following agencies and photographers for granting permission to reproduce the following colour photographs: David Trehane (pp. 17, 23, 27, 32, 47, 52, 53, 56, 60, 63, 68, 70, 74, 78, 79, 82, 83, 86, 88 and 89); Jennifer Trehane (pp. 75 and 77); John Glover (pp. 26, 48 (top and bottom), 49, 57, 61, 71 and 87); Photos Horticultural Picture Library (pp. 12/13, 64, 65 and 90); the Harry Smith Horticultural Photographic Collection (pp. 20/21, 92/93 and 110/111); and Ken Ledward (p. 107). The photograph on pp. 42/43 was taken by Bob Challinor.

All line drawings were drawn by Nils Solberg.